Penguin Education

Penguin Education Specials
General Editor: Willem van der Eyken

Patterns and Policies in Higher Education
George Brosan, Charles Carter, Richard Layard,
Peter Venables, Gareth Williams

Patterns and Policies in Higher Education

George Brosan, Charles Carter,
Richard Layard, Peter Venables,
Gareth Williams

Penguin Books

Penguin Books Ltd, Harmondsworth,
Middlesex, England
Penguin Books Inc., 7110 Ambassador Road,
Baltimore, Md 21207, U.S.A.
Penguin Books Australia Ltd,
Ringwood, Victoria, Australia

First published 1971
Copyright © George Brosan, Charles Carter, Richard Layard,
Peter Venables, Gareth Williams, 1971

Made and printed in Great Britain by
Hazell Watson & Viney Ltd,
Aylesbury, Bucks
Set in Linotype Plantin

Contents

Chapter One
Introduction
Peter Venables

For long regarded as the privilege of the few, and accepted as such by the majority of the population, higher education has now become a central issue for the modern state and its citizens. The desires of one generation are apt to become necessities for succeeding ones, but the time-scale for realizing them has been so radically reduced as to generate an expectation – even a demand – that the necessities be provided well within a lifetime. Cars, and travel generally; shorter hours and more leisure; sport, music, drama and TV sets; increased electrical power per elbow at work and at home: gadgetry galore – and superficially we have a materialist, affluent society. Yet appearances are deceptive. For along with all these gains, and in many respects both a condition and consequence of them, there has been an awareness – uncertain and fitful perhaps, but growing stronger in each decade – that a plethora of goods is not necessarily the good life which will satisfy individual citizens or the community at large. Education is essential to the production of goods and maintenance of services, but it is also vital for maintaining the moral and cultural values which determine how they should be used.

Over the last five years there has been growing apprehension that the rising demands for education might press ever more heavily upon the resources available; indeed, that a severe shortage or a maldistribution of scarce resources might threaten standards and the attainment of excellence, particularly in the universities. These problems were discussed at a conference at Cambridge under the title 'Concepts of Excellence – 1969–1989' (the discussions were reported in *Universities Quarterly*, Summer 1969). A proposal was put forward to produce a book, or perhaps two, on the issues raised at the conference, but there was little agreement about the content. It was felt that it should not be 'full of enormous diagrams and masses of statistics', that it should have 'a genuine theme about what all higher education is in aid of', and that it should not merely be a projection of what is. The issues raised were many and urgent – excellence and relevance; generalist and specialist, vocational and non-vocational education; 'too much "technic" and not enough "poly" '; too much professionalism and no moral commitment; governance, academic autonomy and responsiveness to social needs. It was agreed that most of these issues needed discussion against a firm statistical background, which should be set out as concisely and clearly as possible. At the time of the conference there was a general awareness that the Robbins targets for 1980 would be substantially exceeded, but the magnitude was uncertain. The statistical appraisal became clear late in 1969 (the results are given in Figure 1, p. 21). Before dealing with the broader considerations within which the statistics are to be appraised, a brief comment on the general plan of the book may be of use.

In preliminary discussion there were sharply differing views among the contributors, and it became evident that no single agreed draft would be feasible. On the contrary, provided continuity was secured without overlaps tiresome to the reader, positive advantages might result from the contrasts of differing personal contributions. Thus Charles Carter, George Brosan and the present author, with the advantage of having before us the first draft of chapter 2 by Richard Layard and Gareth Williams, wrote our separate sections on generally agreed outlines, each to a length of about one third of the book. These sections were then compared and analysed, and a single rearranged draft discussed and modified to produce the present structure.

The debate has been taken as far as possible in the time available, but important issues remain unresolved; these are set out in contrasting presentations, or by note and comment. Discussions on the complex, confusing problems of higher education are all too apt to result in the participants finishing in a state which, though perhaps euphoric, is still confused; the present authors hope to have escaped some of the worst hazards, and that our differing presentations will help to clarify the issues and provide a firmer grasp of realities and practicable solutions.

The right to tertiary education

The range of statistical material which underlies chapter 2 was not available to the Robbins Committee at the time of its inquiry (1961 to 1963), and its conclusions were thus comparatively circumscribed and limited. Nevertheless, the uses to which statistics are put depend on wider considerations than the material itself, and interpretation may be influenced by attitudes of mind and values not subject to logical proof. The enthusiastic supporter of a new venture is encouraged by the fact that the theatre appears to be half-full: to the management, burdened by making ends meet, it is undeniably half-empty. The expansion of education beyond school may likewise be viewed enthusiastically as the belated achievement of educational opportunity for all citizens; or be fearfully regarded as a most serious threat to existing standards, so that more must mean worse. Furthermore, it may be felt that Gresham's Law – that bad money drives out good – will apply, and that with expansion the work and the potential of our leading institutions will suffer irretrievably. Before embarking on a detailed consideration of the present system of higher and further education (chapter 3) it is essential to consider what other attitudes are possible, and on what grounds the whole question of the expansion of tertiary education should be determined. Such considerations require a brief historical account of the development of education, and an appraisal of some related social trends. (It should here be explained that, in order to avoid such cumbersome terms as 'higher and further education' and 'education beyond school', the term 'tertiary education' is used in the rest of this chapter, as it follows logically after 'primary' and 'secondary' education. For the greater part, this is education for those aged eighteen years and over, but even after 1972–3 it will still include some of the sixteen- and seventeen-year-olds who will have left school and ceased formally to be part of secondary education. This group will be mentioned specially where the context requires it. This apart, tertiary education, in the post-Latey-Committee age, constitutes the education of adult citizens.)

After decades of dedicated effort, despite adverse conditions, on the part of voluntary bodies, including the churches, the necessity of regular schooling was at last recognized in England by the Education Act of 1870. The extent and quality of that schooling was likewise improved over the succeeding half-century, but it was not until 1944 that, besides primary and secondary education, the provision of further education became a *duty* of the local education authority instead of merely a *power* which might or might not be exercised. Even so, the county colleges which were to provide part-time education for young people in employment aged fifteen, sixteen and seventeen were not established, and part-time, day-release courses grew only gradually over the years. Under the Industrial Training Act of 1964, increasing provision is being made for the part-time training of young people over school-leaving age who are working in industry; that is, for those sixteen years and over as from 1971. Thus over the century since the first Education Act the right of the individual citizen to education has been erratically and reluctantly conceded to the age of sixteen, while opportunities beyond that age have been slowly and patchily provided.

The time is overdue for establishing the right of all citizens to the tertiary education which is appropriate to their proven abilities, irrespective of race, religion, politics and social circumstances. They should have the right to an education which will enable them to develop their innate abilities and qualities, both for their personal fulfilment and for meeting the immensely varied needs of a modern democracy. This right has been even longer delayed than the right to liberty, and yet it is one of liberty's most important safeguards. Those deprived of education are increasingly deprived of opportunity, and of opportunity effectively to exercise other rights. The welfare state embodies the recognition of the citizens' need for minimum standards of health and general welfare; what was formerly granted as an act of grace, and maintained on a voluntary basis, became recognized as a right to be ensured by the State. Likewise the granting of the right to tertiary education is the culmination of the ground-swell of political, educational and social change over a long period of time, and is a fundamental necessity for the next era of development.

From Assent to Consent

We live in turbulent times, with vastly disturbing events and issues brought instantly and insistently into our homes by the mass media. It is difficult not to be daunted by the vast scale and refractory nature of so many present-day problems – political, economic, and social; by cruelty and oppression, illiteracy and inequality of opportunity – the list is desperately formidable. Their significance and their solution are as difficult to grasp and comprehend as space exploration and moon landings must be to a 'flat-earther', and this will continue to be so unless the range and scope of tertiary education is significantly changed, and the right to it is granted. Stripped of their superficialities and irrelevances, however, a great proportion of these events and issues are but manifestations of man's very proper concern with human conditions, with the quality of life not at some distant time, or in the foreseeable future, but within the *attainable* future. In the past, and up to recent times, most of mankind have not been free or able to make their wishes known. Inarticulate, ineffective, and impotent to achieve their objectives, they have been weighed down by cultural, economic and political burdens.

Though the period of change has been immensely long, the effects have been cumulative and mainly irreversible. In interpreting these, and in trying to discern the nature and direction of future trends, a firm basis for understanding and constructive action can be found in the concept that all of us – individuals, society at large, even the nations of the world – are passing from an Age of Assent to an Era of Consent. More accurately, people are feeling their uncertain way forward from an Age of Required Assent – required willy-nilly by economic, political, religious and social pressures – to an Era of Voluntary Consent, given freely out of understanding and consultation: that is, from an Age of Compliance perforce to an Era of Consent perhaps, which is a change not likely to be congenial to those in power.[1]

Of numerous possible examples, a few will suffice to show how widespread is this general trend, and how deeply it affects human

1. Part of this and later chapters by the present author are based on the Birkbeck College Foundation Oration, 'Conflicting patterns and purposes in higher education', reprinted in *Universities Quarterly*, Autumn 1970.

life and society at highly sensitive points of change. There is the slow progress towards modern management in industry and commerce, with its consultative and bargaining procedures, and with proposed contentious legislation to deal with 'wildcat' strikes. Some of the important issues involved were discussed by Professor Kenneth Walker in his recent outstanding lecture on 'Industrial democracy: fantasy, fiction or fact?' (*The Times*, 4 and 5 March 1970). Speaking of firms and businesses as enterprises, Professor Walker stated that:

Both the administrative and engineering views of the enterprise are mistaken, for each confuses a single significant aspect of the enterprise with the whole. Enterprises are in fact *socio-technical systems*, in which human beings are directed towards certain overriding objectives of the enterprise. ... The issue of industrial democracy is essentially whether such *inevitable participation in events* is to be accompanied by *participation in the decisions* intended to guide these events.

Professor Walker concluded his lecture thus:

We are on the brink of a new phase in our thinking about industrial democracy, a phase in which we shall have to give up dogmatic discussion and forsake hunch for research and practical experiment. In this phase we shall cease to take up extreme, unyielding positions which close the debate with all-or-nothing statements preventing any practical progress. Instead, we shall embark on more and more experiments, each taking one more step towards making industrial democracy a fact. How long this process will take, and how painful it will be, will depend on managers, workers and governments. Their skill, their wisdom and their goodwill will need to be strong – as strong as the stubbornness of facts.

And all these, we may add with certainty, will be profoundly influenced and enhanced by the quality of the tertiary education of the future.

We are already within a new phase of thinking and action with regard to the development of our educational institutions, with the progressive participation of staff and students in their governance and academic deliberations. Changes now contemplated or being implemented in the constitution of councils and senates of universities were out of the question less than a decade ago, as were the conditions of governance now granted to colleges and polytechnics as a result of the Weaver Report (1966).

Furthermore, we may think of other social institutions, such as marriage, where we are moving from an unequal dependent relationship to an equality for husband and wife before the law, and towards more humane conditions for divorce and re-marriage. Family planning, family commitments and pleasures, and budgeting are more the common concern of equal partners than was so in the past. At the same time, relationships between parents and their children have changed towards an informality that would have astonished our grandparents. 'Because I say so' are now famous last words for adolescents, and may be felt to betray a regrettable, even an offensive, lack of reason and affection. An informal comradeship which engenders mutual understanding by such needful reason and affection is more apt than authoritarian discipline to help the adolescent to adulthood. Against this background we should no longer underestimate the adverse consequences of the general lack of educational opportunities enjoyed by women. These are so poor, compared with those readily available to men, that one might be justified in thinking tertiary education to be a sex-linked characteristic, highly disadvantageous to women (with recessive genes in Britain, though advantageous, almost dominant genes in the USSR). To deny a woman education 'because she is going to get married' is a cynical denial of a basic human right, and an outstanding example of creating our own headaches and reserving the right to complain.

From Required Assent to Voluntary Consent sums up the long-enduring struggles to change political systems, from the dominance of empires, autocracies, oligarchies and dictatorships to democracies of varying degrees of effectiveness; and sums up, too, the unique transformation of the British Empire into the Commonwealth. One further illustration is in the religious sphere. The ecumenical movement has no significance, and certainly no future, unless it is a movement (however imperceptible at times) away from an Age of Assent, in belief and conforming practice required by authority, to the Era of Consent: consent, that is, which is freely given out of understanding and consultation. Professor Walker's observations about avoiding dogmatic discussion, unyielding positions and painful transitions, and the need for skill, wisdom and goodwill, are pertinent also to the nature and direction of religious change. They apply to the relationship between the various churches and denominations and between the particular churches and their individual members in matters both of belief and conduct.

'Men make institutions, institutions mould men,' said Churchill, but many, if not most, of man's institutions were the product of the Age of Assent, founded by men accustomed to require assent. The traditional moulds are therefore suspect and are no longer automatically acceptable to the rising generation. The change to the Era of Consent is so profound that the most searching and widespread questioning of existing institutions is quite inescapable. To paraphrase an old word-game: 'I show initiative, thou art unpredictable, he is a deviant.' A rebel against the traditional mould is a deviant with a socially inconvenient initiative – but it may be indispensable for progress. Indeed this has been the basis of progress, and the heterodoxy of one generation is apt to become the orthodoxy of the next. So the serious concern of adult students (and most students in tertiary education in the post-Latey-Committee age are adults in law) about the nature of their society – and ours – is to be welcomed, despite the excessive and untoward methods of protest used on occasion.

Moulding constraints are indispensable to the continuity of a civilized society, but its institutions and their moulding purposes need to be understood and modified in response to the changing needs and aspirations of mankind. Formerly, the slow rate of change enabled the moulds to be turned to developing needs at a reasonably commensurate rate. Now the pace and character of change induced by science and technology produce problems which cannot be contained or solved within the traditional moulds, and the resulting stresses and strains put a premium on understanding and communication. Education is perforce the basis of a technological society, but tertiary education is no less an indispensable defence against its abuses. 'Power always tends to corrupt, absolute power corrupts absolutely,' said Acton. Technological power can all too readily become an absolutely corrupting power, as the last three decades right up to the present time bear frequent and terrible witness. The prevention of abuses and the solution of problems belong wholly to adult citizenship.

Tertiary education, which comprises the intellectual, vocational, physical, emotional, political and philosophical education of adult citizens, is from now on of critical importance to the well-being of democracy.

In the Age of Assent education was a privilege of relatively few individuals, but under economic and organizational pressures it became increasingly a necessity to be provided by the State. The poorly educated, inadequately trained individual increasingly became a liability, a casualty in peace and war; a fact which compelled a reluctant but slowly increasing investment in education by governments the world over. As the benefits of education become more widely evident, more positive attitudes are beginning to prevail, but resistance to the further changes that are still required for the Era of Consent diminishes all too slowly.

The Age of Assent is the age of restricted educational opportunity, with attitudes characterized, if more education is suggested, by such questions as 'Where are the labourers to come from?' By contrast, the Era of Consent must inherently be the era of expansion and diversification of educational opportunity. More means different, and perhaps very different, but different does not necessarily mean worse. On the contrary, more may mean better for the great majority of young people. The labouring and unpleasant service work will increasingly be done with the aid of 'mechanical slaves' and electronic servo-mechanisms, with increased education and training for those who design, manufacture, sell *and* use them. For the Age of Assent the educational system is the minimum sanitary provision commensurate with draining away ignorance sufficiently so that a complex society will somehow cohere and manage to get by. For the Era of Consent the educational provision is the maximum attainable to sustain a creative, progressive, satisfying democratic society.

The emergence and establishment of a right can be seriously inhibited, if not entirely prevented, by the inertia of long-established attitudes of mind. When, in succeeding generations, the particular right has been won and accepted as normal, the inhibiting attitudes and limitations seem well-nigh incomprehensible. This is true of the long struggle for the emancipation of slaves, the bargaining rights of workers, and universal suffrage.

The more developed a society is, the more sophisticated and subtle become the ways in which defensive attitudes exert their influence. Thus recently we have seen arguments for maintaining quality, versus allowing increased quantity, dressed up to deceive the very elect, so that those charged with the duty of providing education seek to diminish or restrict its bountiful influence. As for the expansion of tertiary education now required, that is, the Robbins Report 'target' figures plus a forty per cent over-shoot (chapter 2), with the inevitable changes of pattern, the academic world is by no means exempt from these attitudes. That any change from the traditional pattern is bound to be a change for the worse is apt to be a traditional academic reaction, and especially towards expansion. Adherence to tradition then becomes defence in depth against change, and this may be a characteristic of a whole society still firmly set in the Age of Assent. The investigations of A. H. Halsey and Martin Trow are particularly significant in this regard.[1]

The apprehension of British academics regarding expansion – of the system, their own subjects, their departments and universities – is, we suggest, a fear of the future. And what is feared is not 'a deterioration of the quality of my students' so much as the unknown problems that significant expansion may bring with it. To many British academic men, expansion is the source of threat, of unanticipated and undesired consequences, of dangers rather than of challenge and opportunity.

The fear of the future, if we are right, is one reflection of a central quality of British society just now, which shows itself more widely as a fear of modernization, automation, immigration, Americanization, of all sorts of processes which have unknown outcomes. The British, including the academic community, will accept 'reforms' if they believe they know or can foresee the controlled extent and consequences of change. The society is in this sense cautious, and exhibits the characteristic stance and mood of an economy of scarcity. This is what it means to call it a deeply conservative society: the extraordinary wariness and resistance to large-scale expansion of the system of higher education on the part of academics is one aspect of this mood and stance.

1. A. H. Halsey and M. Trow, *The British Academics*, Faber, 1970, and M. A. Trow and A. H. Halsey, 'Attitudes to expansion', *Higher Education Review*, Autumn 1969.

The fears exemplified by Halsey and Trow are reinforced strongly by another, the fear of the loss of authority. This fear is of course not confined to academics but is widespread among managers and parents, and there is indeed a deep-seated resistance in the body politic to the change from Assent to Consent. This results in overt repressive actions and rapidly changing attitudes: for example, a reaction to student demonstrations soon surfaces as a generalized hostility to universities.

The recognition of the right to tertiary education must not be frustrated either by entrenched attitudes or by fears of the future. Without the exercise and fulfilment of this right other rights will be eroded, responsibilities hampered or neglected, and creative energies misdirected. Hooliganism and other social disorders are not so much signs of unoriginal sin as the effects of boredom and frustration, arising especially from the cumulative erosion of the rights of the individual.

Chapter Two
The Scale of Expansion to Come

The previous chapter speaks of a 'right to tertiary education' which should not be frustrated. Such generalities bring a predictable reaction from those who regard themselves as 'practical men': 'Exactly what does this mean, in terms of numbers, of effort, of resources diverted from other desirable purposes?' So, before we started to plan the rest of the book, the group of authors asked Richard Layard and Gareth Williams to illuminate by statistics the ground that we are standing on. Their discussions on the scale of expansion does not, however, show the consequences of allowing a general right to tertiary education, for this seems to be too difficult an object to achieve in a decade; it has the more limited aim of showing the consequences if it is decided that there should be no *increase* in the proportion of applicants who have to be disappointed of a place in higher education. This is a very modest aim for a developed country, but, such is the success of the secondary education programme, it turns out nevertheless to involve considerably increased numbers and substantial cost. Richard Layard and Gareth Williams return to the ways of alleviating the cost problem in chapter 8; this chapter simply sets out the best current estimates of numbers and costs, derived from the work of the Higher Education Research Unit at the London School of Economics, and relates the projected expansion to manpower needs. It is based on extrapolation of existing figures and takes no account of any hidden demand.

Richard Layard and
Gareth Williams[1]

How will the revolution of rising expectations affect the demand for higher education, and how should the government respond? In this chapter we try to estimate the demand and to put forward a costed plan of response based on the 'Robbins principle' that higher education should grow in proportion to the demand for it. Some people believe this is the wrong approach, and that expansion should be tuned to the demand for trained manpower rather than to students' demands for places. Even if this were desirable, it is unfortunately still impossible with existing knowledge to forecast the demand for manpower in, say, ten years' time. But manpower issues are clearly important, and in the last section of the chapter (see p. 39) we speculate on whether all the extra graduates we propose will be fruitfully employed.

We want, first, to know how much full-time higher education will be needed if opportunities for 'qualified school-leavers' are to remain as good (or bad) as they are now.[2] This involves a mixture of prediction and prescription, and we shall concentrate as much on the issues involved in making each as on the actual numbers thrown up. The prediction concerns the future output of qualified school-leavers, and the policy prescription says what

1. We should like to thank Alan Ward, who did the calculations, Peter Armitage and Alice Crampin, who gave helpful advice based on their parallel work on educational models, and the Department of Education and Science (DES), which has financed the Higher Education Research Unit's work on educational models. Details of the sources of the statistics are available from the authors at the London School of Economics, on request.

2. The definition of higher education we are using is that used by the Robbins Committee; that is, broadly, degree and teacher-training courses, and further education beyond GCE 'A' level or the Ordinary National Certificate. 'Tertiary education' (see p. 9) is a wider term, which embraces all education beyond school. For definitions of the terms used in this chapter, and a discussion of the factors affecting the demand for higher education, see R. Layard, J. King and C. Moser, *The Impact of Robbins*, Penguin, 1969. For the Robbins Committee's projections see Committee on Higher Education, *Higher Education*, HMSO, Cmnd 2154, ch. 6.

proportion of these should go into each type of higher education and for how long.

Qualified school-leavers

The government has been publishing (in the annual *Statistics of Education*) regular predictions of GCE output ever since the Robbins Report. These present a melancholy tale of under-estimation, as Figure 1 shows, and the story is worth rehearsing

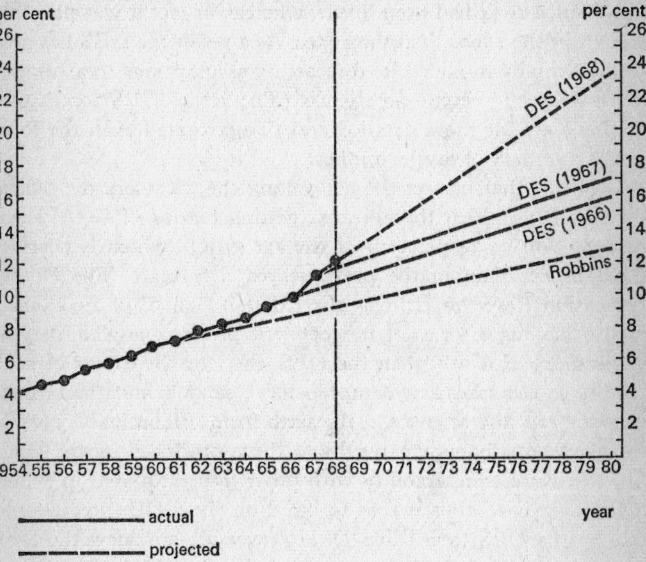

Figure 1 Percentage of the age group obtaining two or more 'A' levels

briefly so as to set the present forecast in perspective. The Robbins Committee estimated that by 1980 the proportion of the age group obtaining two or more 'A' levels would be 12·9 per cent – compared with 6·9 per cent in 1961 and 4·3 per cent in 1954. This implied that the future trend would be slightly less steep than the linear trend from 1954 to 1961, and partly for this reason the Robbins Committee said the forecast gave a minimum estimate of demand. It did indeed prove to be too low – by the very first year of the forecast period. (Though the

Robbins Report was published in 1963 the actual data on 1962 were not yet available, and were therefore forecast.) The same has been true of almost every forecast since, as is illustrated by the two DES forecasts shown in Figure 1 as DES (1966) and DES (1967). The years referred to are the latest years for which actual data were available at the time of the forecast, and in each case the forecasts for the next year (1967 and 1968 respectively) were strikingly exceeded. It is easy, using hindsight, to see why these forecasts went wrong: they implied essentially that the trend since 1954 had been linear, whereas in fact it was palpably steeper in the 1960s than the 1950s. As a result the DES has now fundamentally modified its forecasting assumptions so as to give more weight to recent experience. (The actual DES forecasting methods are far more detailed and disaggregated than the foregoing summary of results implies.)

It is this that has set the cat among the pigeons: the official forecast is now that the numbers getting two or more 'A' levels in 1980 will be 24 per cent of the age group, which is nearly a third higher than in the previous year's forecast. The Higher Education Research Unit at the London School of Economics is also making a series of independent projections which try to allow more explicitly than the DES ones for the effects of such factors as the spread of comprehensive schools and the balance between arts and sciences in the sixth form. Preliminary work so far gives broadly similar results to those produced by the DES. So, to ensure comparability with other figures quoted in public debate, we have chosen here to build on the GCE forecasts put out by the DES (see Table 1). However, in our view the forecast is more likely to prove too low than too high. It assumes that the growth in staying on at school ceases to be exponential in 1971 and becomes linear thereafter. Nor does it allow explicitly for any effect on sixth-form development of the raising of the school-leaving age to sixteen in 1972. Such influences are very difficult to quantify, but could easily make the figures we use here into substantial underestimates.[1]

1. See A. Crampin and P. Armitage, 'The pressure of numbers: speculation for the seventies', *Higher Education Review*, Spring 1970. They speculate that this might add nearly 20 per cent to the output of qualified leavers.

Table 1

Percentage of the Age Group Obtaining 'A' Levels

No. of 'A' levels	1956	1961	1966	1968	1976	1981
Two or more	4·8	6·9	9·6	11·8	20·0	24·5
One	1·5	2·1	3·2	4·1	6·7	8·6

Before we go on to build on these forecasts, two obvious questions arise. First, if all the forecasts have been so wrong before, what is the point of forecasting at all? This is to miss the whole point of the exercise. Forecasting is not an academic pursuit to be judged by whether it gives rise to true or false propositions. It is an operational exercise, to be judged by whether it gives rise to better decisions than would have been taken without it. So long as there is planning, that is to say, an organized attempt to achieve consistency between the activities of different agents, there must be forecasting. Each forecast is provisional, and the most we can hope for is that our provisional ideas at any point in time are the best that could have been formed in the circumstances. The best estimate is that which enables the government most closely to fulfil its policy on educational opportunity and to provide whatever is offered at least (discounted) cost. Thus, for a given eventual student population, too high a forecast could cause empty space, while too low a one might lead to excessive costs of crash construction and of teaching in inappropriate buildings.

One reason why past forecasts have gone wrong is that they did not allow for their own effects. If demand in one period is met as a result of the forecast, demand in the next period will be higher than it otherwise would have been : what is true of urban roads is equally true of higher education.[1] But this in no way invalidates the objective of meeting the demand as it arises.

1. For a discussion of the persistent tendency of forecasts to underestimate the demand for higher education in Western European countries, see G. L. Williams, 'Educational policies, plans and forecasts during the nineteen-sixties and seventies', in *Conference on Policies for Educational Growth, Background Study No. 5*, OECD Committee for Scientific and Technical Personnel.

A second question that gets raised is: Why 'A' levels? Everyone knows that 'A' level often reflects quite inadequately an individual's suitability for higher education, and in any case the 'A' level exam may have disappeared by 1980. However, these objections are based on a misunderstanding. We are not concerned with discriminating between one individual and another, but with deciding on a suitable total number of students. Nor are we interested in projecting 'A' levels as such. What we need to know is the future rate of growth of the pool from which higher education entrants should be drawn. And all we are claiming is that in the past the rate of growth of 'A' levels has corresponded to the rate of growth of suitably qualified people. That is why we project this rate of growth. It is of course possible that a new pattern of examinations will accelerate or retard the rate of growth of the pool, but this does not invalidate attempts to project it under 'A' level nameplates.

Entry to higher education and the binary issue

The next step is to decide what proportion of people with each level of school-leaving qualification should have higher education available for them, and what sort of higher education it should be. The Robbins Committee laid down two principles: that the proportions of people with each given GCE level entering full-time higher education (as a whole) should not fall and, where possible, should rise; and similarly for the proportions entering university. The argument was that as a matter of fact the proportions *applying* were unlikely to fall, and that as a matter of value the proportions of applicants *accepted* ought not to fall. Stiffer competition for places, they argued, would result in personal unhappiness and frustration, and encourage cramming rather than education in the sixth form. These arguments seem to us as valid now as then.

Most people would accept them for higher education as a whole. But there is disagreement on whether they apply equally to the universities. Within the universities, there are those who believe that expansion at the rate implied must lead to a decline in standards.[1] The evidence of degree performance in past expansions does not support this argument, nor the evidence on

1. See Halsey and Trow, *The British Academics*.

the measured scholastic aptitudes of US students during the even more rapid expansion in that country.[1]

A second argument for reducing the universities' share of the higher-education cake comes from the protagonists of the 'binary policy'. Ideally, in our conception, the question of the universities' share would be an irrelevance, since the universities would be closely linked to the colleges of education through university schools of education (as in Robbins), and to the polytechnics through shared facilities and teaching arrangements and through common degrees. However, the government's binary policy has been devised otherwise, and this makes the question of shares an important one. The basic aim of the binary policy is to create a 'public' sector of higher education, separate from but having 'parity of esteem' with the universities. This has often seemed to imply that the public sector should grow in size relative to the universities. The main arguments advanced for the policy have been:

1. The manpower argument, that only thus can applied studies be adequately developed.

2. The social argument, alleging that universities deter students from working-class homes, by their unappealing ethos and their emphasis on GCE entry qualifications.

3. The institutional argument, that polytechnics can be more comprehensive than universities, by including part-time and sub-degree-level as well as degree-level courses.

4. The cost argument, that universities necessarily cost more, because their teachers insist on being paid from university funds for doing research as well as teaching.

All these arguments appeal to valid dissatisfactions with present arrangements. But one cannot help doubting whether the binary policy is likely to prove the right way to remedy the ills concerned. If teachers who research also have time to write more books (including textbooks) and become better known than teachers who do not, the polytechnics will find it difficult to achieve parity of attraction for students, especially when the government drags its feet over elementary steps such as equalizing salary prospects for staff (which requires a full share of professorial posts in polytechnics). And if parity of esteem is not achieved, how can

1. See Robbins, Appendix One, pp. 84–8.

the polytechnics confer status on applied studies – which, we argue later, is a much more serious problem than any supposed quantitative shortage on that side?

Moreover the cost argument is much less clear than is sometimes suggested. Unfortunately the DES have not put out any figures on costs in polytechnics. But they are believed to have been allowing for a difference of only about a hundred pounds between costs per student in polytechnics and in universities. The only calculation we have been able to do is for advanced further education as a whole. This gives a current cost per 'fulltime equivalent' student-year in further education in 1966–7 of £675, as against £875 in universities.[1] There are notorious difficulties in interpreting this kind of evidence. The further-education figure does not isolate either the polytechnics or degree-level work, nor does it relate to the same subject-mix as in universities. There is also a great variation of costs between institutions, which the figure fails to reveal. The university figure includes a good deal of expenditure on research – it consists of all university expenditure (other than the 12 per cent financed by research grants) divided by the number of students. It thus includes the salaries of all teaching staff, who may spend as much as a half of their time on research, and of most technicians and secretaries. (Of course if the research is valueless apart from its effects on the quality of teaching, all these university costs should be attributed to the students, but this seems a rather extreme assumption.) One could also argue that the true product of teaching is not 'student-years', but 'graduated students', in which case the much higher dropout rates in further education could greatly raise their relative unit cost. However, when it comes to capital provision, there is a notorious gap between universities and further education. This is what hits the eye, but, as we shall point out later, capital costs amount to a much smaller proportion of costs than is often imagined.

Why is further education not cheaper than it is, relative to

---

1. See Table 5 (p. 37). The DES Planning Paper, *Student Numbers in Higher Education in England and Wales* (1970), has a slightly lower estimate of unit costs in advanced further education. The main difference is that the DES was able to take out loan charges on the basis of information not available to us.

universities? Arithmetically one can say that it is because the student–staff ratio is rather lower than in universities (in 1961–2 it was 5 : 7 as against 7 : 5), and because average salaries are not so much lower as one might expect, owing to the need to pay younger staff of given qualifications as much as £500 more than in universities in order to retain them. The student–staff ratio is low, of course, because of the smaller average enrolment per course and because of the long hours which each student spends being taught. Both these things are in principle alterable, though small courses will continue to sprout until the DES requires the polytechnics to submit development plans which restrict flexibility to the margin where it belongs, instead of permitting it to pervade the whole system.

We are not arguing against the rapid development of the polytechnics. There is an important role for institutions more closely linked with the world of employment than some universities seem willing to be, and for institutions that specifically cater for part-timers as well as full-timers. Moreover, the competition may improve the universities, though up to now it has been competition from the 'new' universities which has jogged the old ones, more than from the polytechnics or even the former colleges of advanced technology.[1] However, the issue which concerns us here is not whether the public sector should flourish and multiply, which given the general pace of expansion it cannot fail to do, but whether it should do so in a way that reduces the proportion of well-qualified school-leavers who go to university. For the reasons we have given, we think not. The available evidence is that sixth-formers want to go to university as much as before, and this means that the neglect of applied studies, of working-class opportunity and of reasonable economy must be tackled in the universities themselves as well as outside.

The validity of the last sentence is not upset by the Kent Education Committee's survey of 1,599 Kent sixth-form leavers entering full-time higher education in 1968, which showed that 45 per cent went to university, 8 per cent 'entered non-university institutions because they could not get places at a university' and 47 per cent entered non-university institutions

1. See H. J. Perkin, *New Universities in the United Kingdom*, OECD, Paris, 1969.

'as their first choice' (*The Times Educational Supplement*, 13 March 1970, p. 14). That these results (regularly quoted by Gerry Fowler, the former Minister of State for Higher Education) are entirely atypical is shown by the following results of the Brunel University survey.[1] Of a random sample of about 1,800 sixth-formers in England and Wales studying for 'A' levels who said they intended to go on to further full-time education, 70 per cent wanted to go to university, 17·5 per cent to colleges of education, 10 per cent to further education and 2·5 per cent to other institutions. It is also interesting that of about 26,500 school leavers in 1968 who had what the DES defined as 'two or more high-grade "A" level passes' and proceeded to further full-time study, 90 per cent went to university, 4 per cent to colleges of education and 6 per cent to further education (*Statistics of Education 1968*, part 2).

We are now in a position to make our projection of entrants. Table 2 shows what proportion of those with each number of

Table 2

Home Initial Entrants to Full-Time Higher Education as Percentage of 'A' Level Output (Entrants for England and Wales, 1967)

No. of 'A' levels	Universities	Colleges of education	Further education	No full-time higher education	All with GCE
Two or more	59	16	7	18	100
One	—	32	18	50	100

'A' levels went to full-time higher education in 1967 – 82 per cent of those with two or more 'A' levels (including 59 per cent who went to university) and 50 per cent of those with one 'A' level.[2] These 'A' level entrants numbered 79,000 in all, and there

1. See M. Kaneti-Barry, R. Baldy and W. van der Eyken, *2,100 Sixth-Formers*, Hutchinson, 1971.

2. The figures for further education are very approximate, and probably somewhat understate the proportion of GCE-holders going to that sector, since they assume that the pattern of qualifications in further education in 1967 was the same as in 1961. This does not substantially affect the projection, since it leads to an equivalent overestimate of the number of entrants without GCE.

were 26,000 other entrants, divided fairly between colleges of education (mostly with five or more 'O' levels) and further education (mostly with Ordinary National Certificates).

Given our assumptions, the projection is now easy. The total entry to all higher education in each future year should equal 82 per cent of those with two or more 'A' levels and 50 per cent of those with one 'A' level only. For those without 'A' level we assume a constant number of entrants – the DES projection of the output of people with 'O' level but no 'A' level is roughly constant for the future, and the numbers with ONC are not growing either. The assumption of constant numbers of entrants to higher education here may be conservative, and lends force to our feeling that the projection we give ought to be considered a minimum.

What of the division of entrants between the different sectors? University entry, we asume, continues at 59 per cent of two or more 'A' levels. (This is roughly equivalent to the figure used in the 1970 DES Planning Paper, *Student Numbers in Higher Education in England and Wales*.) As between colleges of education and further education, our procedure is entirely arbitrary and intended as much as anything to bring out the lack of realism in the present DES policy, on which our projection for colleges of education is based. The DES paper projects the number of places in colleges of education in England and Wales at 124,000 in 1976–7 and 130,000 in 1981–2, these figures being based on the estimated demand for teaching manpower and not on students' demands for places in the colleges. This policy involves a very narow view of the role of the colleges and there seems to be no good reason why these figures, which imply very little growth from now on, should be at all relevant if the colleges develop into major centres of social work training or, some of them, into liberal arts colleges, as is suggested in chapter 8. However, it does not seem likely that the colleges of education will develop a lot less fast than the polytechnics and other colleges of further education, and so for the sake of illustration only we use the DES projection.

Student numbers and courses

From home entrants it is a small step to places for home students.
In further education we assume a constant 'effective length of
course' of 3·2 years. In colleges of education we assume that
the proportion taking four-year courses for a B.Ed. rises from
15 per cent of the intake in 1970 to 40 per cent of the intake in
the later 1970s. This should be quite practicable if the rise in
quality of entrants forecast (p. 35) comes about, but this in turn
may well depend on some broadening in the scope of the colleges.
In universities there is the problem of the effect of the growth
of postgraduate study. For example in England and Wales, excluding the former CATs, the effective length of course rose
from 3·65 years in 1961–2 to 3·81 in 1966–7.[1] The undergraduate
component of this was roughly constant at 3·1 years over the
period, but the postgraduate component rose sharply. What
should we assume for the future? There are those who think that
postgraduate education has mushroomed too fast, especially in
the natural sciences, and the University Grants Committee in the
last quinquennium took the view that 'undergraduate numbers
are a genuine priority'. However it seems most unlikely that we
shall see a reversal of the long-standing tendency, observed in so
many different countries, for the higher levels of education to
grow faster than the lower. In Britain this is especially unlikely
if we allow for the introduction of compulsory teacher training
for graduate schoolteachers in the early 1970s, and for the rapid
growth of post-experience courses. Thus a minimum projection
would assume a constant effective length of course, which is our
basic assumption. A maximum projection might assume that the
effective length of course continued to grow at the same linear
rate as between 1961–2 and 1966–7: this would imply 70,000
more university places in 1981–2 than the minimum assumption. What actually happens is likely to lie between these extremes.

There are two further steps. One is to allow for places for
students from Scotland, which we do by assuming they increase at the same rate as students from England and Wales.
This may be too low, but alternative assumptions would make

---

1. Layard *et al.*, *The Impact of Robbins*, p. 117.

little difference to the Great Britain total. The second, and more problematical, is to allow for overseas students. The Robbins Committee said that one should expect these to increase at the same rate as home students. This has not happened. Overseas student numbers have grown, but less than half as fast as home student numbers. From 1962–3 to 1966–7 the average annual growth was 540 (or 4 per cent a year simple interest) in universities, 630 (or 14 per cent simple interest) in further education, and zero in colleges of education. These are nevertheless substantial rates of growth, especially considering the domestic pressure on places at the time. To assume no growth from now on would be unnecessarily conservative and insular. There is no reason to expect the forces that have produced past growth to become less powerful in future. It is true that in the year or two after 1966–7 there was little growth, owing to the increase in overseas students' fees made by Anthony Crosland, then Secretary of State for Education. But this is something which one would expect to affect the level of the number of students once and for all, rather than its long-run rate of growth over time. Indeed, given peace and increased interdependence between nations, and the possible entry of Britain into the Common Market, one might expect the growth of international student migration between advanced countries to accelerate, with Britain a net gainer of students due to its attractions for North American students. As regards students coming to Britain from developing countries, their number depends mainly on the extent of educational provision in their own countries, and on the availability of finance for them to study in Britain. The period since 1966 has not been a good one for British overseas aid, but hopefully things are improving. Educational development abroad, though it may possibly reduce the demand for undergraduate places in Britain, will vastly raise the demand for postgraduate places. We have, therefore, allowed for the continued growth of overseas student numbers in universities and further education at the same linear rate as from 1962–3 to 1966–7.

And so at last, in Table 3, we arrive at our projection of places. (It may be wondered why, given the uncertainties involved and the different policy options available, we only give one projection. The answer is that in the available space it would be

Table 3

Students in Full-Time Higher Education in Great Britain (in thousands)

	Universities	Colleges of education	Further education	All full-time higher education
Actual				
1959/60	104	38	28	170
1966/7	184	95	60	339
1967/8	200	106	70	376
1968/9	212	120	83	415
1969/70*	225	126	92	443
Projection				
1972/3	267	132	102	501
1973/4	281	133	109	523
1974/5	298	134	120	552
1975/6	317	135	132	584
1976/7	340	136	145	621
1977/8	365	137	159	661
1978/9	390	138	175	703
1979/80	417	140	191	748
1980/1	446	142	208	796
1981/2	477	144	226	847

*Estimates (by DES).

confusing to attempt more, but the results of the main permutations can be easily imagined.) It indicates a total full-time enrolment of 847,000 students by 1981–2, of whom 477,000 would be in universities, 144,000 in colleges of education, and 226,000 in advanced further education. These total enrolments are 52 per cent higher than the Robbins projections for that year. They corespond closely to the numbers in the 1970 DES projection of *Student Numbers in Higher Education in England and Wales*, though there are some differences in the assumptions made. The DES assume that the proportion of qualified school-leavers entering higher education would be as in the early 1960s rather than as now, which makes for a higher projection, but they also assume no growth in overseas students, which makes for a lower projection.

The conclusion is that, unless there is a radical change in educational policy, we must expect to see higher education grow by at least 70 per cent in the 1970s. When compared with the growth of 160 per cent in the 1960s this seems quite modest, and the absolute increase between 1969–70 and 1979–80 is only 32,000 more than that in the previous ten-year period. This makes it all the more necessary to stress that the projection is likely to be a minimum of what is needed – it allows nothing for the raising of the school-leaving age, for increasing proportions of postgraduates, or for a host of influences that could lead to many more places being needed.

Given these broad totals, innumerable questions arise about the structure of education in each sector. We shall comment on only three issues. In universities the crucial issue is the balance between subjects. It is exceptionally difficult to forecast the balance between arts and science in the school output, especially when the introduction of new school-leaving exams may do much to prevent this unnecessary dichotomy. Historically there was at 'A' level a swing to science in the 1950s, followed by the notorious swing to arts in the 1960s. This led the Dainton Committee into some lugubrious forecasts (by extrapolation) of the supply of potential scientists, which were always implausible and have already been falsified, as Table 4 shows. In 1968 and 1969 there seems to have been no marked shift one way or the other between arts and science. Doubtless the balance of sixth-formers' choices is partly affected by the relative supply of places in higher education, the present relative ease of entry in science having helped to stem the swing to arts. Thus the balance of the demand for places as between arts and science is probably a good deal more dependent on government policy than is the size of the total demand for places. But in the long run the main influence is likely to be the evolution of the labour market. The notion that 'the increasingly technological character of our society' requires an increasing proportion of our graduates to be professional scientists or technologists is widespread but undemonstrable. Economic development certainly requires a good level of mathematical competence and general scientific knowledge among all educated people, which is why the present shortage of maths and science schoolteachers is so disturbing. (Such a

Table 4
Percentage of First-Year Sixth-Formers Studying Arts and Science in England and Wales

	Science group	Science-cum-arts group	Arts group	All
Actual				
1962	41·5	9·9	48·6	100·0
1967	31·4	15·8	52·8	100·0
1968	30·1	17·1	52·8	100·0
1969	30·0	18·6	51·4	100·0
Dainton projection*				
1969	27·5	17·7	54·8	100·0
1971	23·5	20·1	56·4	100·0

*The Dainton projection was based on 'actuals' up to and including 1967.

shortage could, of course, act as a constraint on the numbers of sixth-formers qualified to study scientific subjects in university.) But professional education in science is very expensive (see p. 37) and requires a type of mental discipline which imposes a heavy psychic cost on many students who may yet wish to raise their general level of education. For this reason it is not surprising that in the US only about 20 per cent of Bachelor's degree graduates major in science and technology, and that no major advanced country has experienced a substantial swing to science in higher education in the last fifteen years.[1] It seems safe therefore to expect the broad arts/science balance in universities in 1980 to look fairly much as now, hopefully with less specialization, more social studies and relatively less literature.

In colleges of education the type of curriculum will depend partly on the supply and demand situation in the primary schools, which is rapidly improving, and partly on the quality of their students. If they expand their intake by as little as we

1. See C. M. Phillips, *Changes in Subject Choice in School and University*, Weidenfeld & Nicolson, 1969.

have assumed and if they always select their best-qualified applicants, then the proportion of entrants with two or more 'A' levels will rise from 36 per cent in 1967 to 85 per cent in 1981. The radical implications of this are particularly obvious when one considers that recent improvements in the quality of education in the colleges have been accompanied by no significant improvement in the qualifications of entrants – 34 per cent had two or more 'A' levels in 1958. On reflection it seems most unlikely that this change could come about, that the colleges could maintain their drawing power relative to the polytechnics, unless they broadened their courses and made them less specifically tied to teaching as a career. The other important implication of the change would be that a major avenue of opportunity for girls with one 'A' level or with 'O' levels only would have been cut off. According to our projection, these people will go into further education, where they will presumably take courses in social work, commercial subjects and the like. This may be all right, but it is a point which those in the colleges of education ought to be aware of.

In further education a major issue is the relative role of the thirty polytechnics and of the other colleges. At present the polytechnics accommodate about half the advanced full-time students in further education. According to the White Paper (Cmnd 3006, 1966) the polytechnics were to grow to 2,000 full-time students each, making 60,000 in all. This would have been a quite inadequate contribution to the total demand for places in further education, and targets like 5,000 each seem to be nearer the mark. However, judging by the experience of the CATs,[1] it is not easy for existing institutions to change their role and grow rapidly at the same time – especially if they are intended not to shed their part-time work. The role of the other colleges therefore seems assured. But the vital thing is that, faced with the scale of change that confronts it, the government should make a ten-year plan for higher education, including a ten-year plan for each institution. Even in further education the traditional evolutionary approach will not do. Without a plan the costs of the impending expansion will be astronomical.

1. See T. Burgess and J. Pratt, *Policy and Practice: The Colleges of Advanced Technology*, Allen Lane The Penguin Press, 1970.

The costs will in any case be heavy. In this chapter we forecast what would be needed on present standards of provision. This means – assuming that the inputs per student will remain constant – that there will be fixed staff–student ratios, electricity consumption per student, square-footage per student, and so on.

Cost per student-year

The first step is to estimate the present cost to society of educating each student for a year. This consists of the direct cost of his tuition, together with the indirect cost involved because the student himself is not working in the labour force. The direct cost consists of the current cost (of teachers' salaries and the like) together with the cost of the capital stock (of buildings and equipment) which the student uses. Even if there were no new buildings going up, there would still be a capital cost, as the buildings have alternative uses; we therefore measure the capital cost by the annual rental value of the buildings and equipment used, rather than by the cost of new construction. The indirect cost can be measured roughly by the forgone earnings which students would have earned had they been working, on the assumption that these earnings correspond roughly to the value of what they would have produced. Students' maintenance grants are not a social cost, since they reflect no real loss of output but merely a transfer of purchasing power from non-students to students.

In 1966–7 the average direct social cost of one year's university education was already about £1,075, of which £875 was direct current expenditure and £200 the rental value of buildings and equipment (see Table 5). The indirect cost of earnings forgone was about £700 – somewhat less than the direct cost, but still substantial.

Public funds paid for about 90 per cent of the direct current expenditure and also for most of the capital cost. By contrast the students carried most of the earnings forgone, average maintenance grants for UK students being £270.[1] If we add to-

---

1. Here and throughout we ignore the rental cost of university- and college-owned residential accommodation, which is normally provided free of charge to students. The reason is that it seems likely that little additional residential accommodation will be subsidized. Since we shall shortly assume

gether the average annual public subsidy to a university student's education, it comes to £1,250 – a sobering thought when compared to a male manual worker's average wage (in 1966–7) of £1,050 a year.

Table 5
Direct Cost per Student-Year in Full-Time Higher Education 1966–7

| | Current | | | |
	Salaries and wages	Other	Annual value of capital	Total in £
University				
Arts and				
Social Studies	387	281	109	777
Science	547	411	251	1,209
Technology	650	399	326	1,375
Medical subjects	947	519	251	1,717
All subjects	536	339	201	1,076
Colleges of				
education	357		109	466
Further				
education	673		201	874

There are substantial differences between subjects in their direct cost. Whereas arts and social studies cost about £775 per student-year, the cost rises to £1,200 for science, £1,375 for technology and over £1,700 for medicine. This means that further social investment in, say, technology rather than arts or social studies is only justified if it yields substantially higher benefits. If subsequent wage differences adequately measured the differences in benefits, these would need to average £100 a year over a

that the average costs quoted in Table 5 will also be the marginal costs of future expansion, it seemed best to ignore a cost item for which the marginal cost to public funds will be very low. Students' residence (including lodgings which students pay for) may of course impose a significant marginal *social* cost if students consume more residential accommodation than workers, but there is no obvious way of estimating this.

person's lifetime to justify giving preference to expansion in technology. (This figure is the annual payment needed to repay the £1,800 cost difference (3 × £600) at a 5 per cent interest rate over forty years.)

We have already discussed the comparative cost of universities and further education. The striking point about the non-university sector is the relatively low cost of tuition in colleges of education, arising mainly from their concentration on arts subjects, where student–staff ratios are fairly high in all sectors and where there are low costs of materials and technical assistance.

Total future cost

In projecting future costs we meet a familiar difficulty. We should like to measure the cost in terms of a number of standard 'baskets' of other goods and services which society forgoes by undertaking higher education. This is why we want to measure the cost at constant prices rather than at whatever money prices happen to prevail from year to year. The difficulty is that the cost of the inputs in terms of such standard 'baskets' does not remain constant. It is reasonable to suppose that the 'real' cost of the physical input, such as buildings, electricity and so on, do on average remain constant, but the cost of people (teachers, technicians, secretaries, porters) palpably rises as real wages rise. So if the input of such people per student remains constant, the real cost per student will rise. For this reason faster economic growth can do little to reduce the share of the gross national product (GNP) going to higher education, since costs as well as the GNP rise faster, though faster growth can of course make a given share of public expenditure in the GNP more socially tolerable. In our calculations we assume that the real cost per person employed in higher education rises by $2\frac{1}{2}$ per cent a year, but that students' maintenance grants remain constant in real terms.

We can now combine our assumptions about changing unit costs with our projected student numbers to estimate the total direct social costs of expansion. In principle, as we said before, we ought to include in the cost the loss of students' production, since this is just as definite a cost as the loss of production in other industries reflected in the wages paid to teachers, porters and other employees in higher education. However, because there is no money flow corresponding to students' production forgone, it is conventional to omit this item from cost projections, and we do the same. We are left with the direct current cost, plus the annual rental of capital. In 1966–7 this was £294 million, or 0·87 per cent of the GNP (see Table 6). Most of this comes from public funds, and in addition students' maintenance grants cost about £95 million, or 0·28 per cent of the GNP. The tuition cost in 1981–2, assuming constant inputs per student, will have risen to the astronomical total of £950 million, or 1·8 per cent of the GNP (if the GNP has until then risen by 3 per cent per year), to which should be added £240 million for maintenance grants.

Table 6
Total Cost of Full-Time Higher Education at 1966–7 Prices of Goods and Services

| | *£ million* | | |
	1966–7	*1976–7*	*1981–2*
Direct cost			
University	198	416	628
College of education	44	73	83
Further education	52	146	246
Total	294	635	957
As % of GNP	0·87	1·39	1·81
Maintenance grants	96	177	240
As % of GNP	0·28	0·38	0·45

These costs are enormous, and raise vital questions about whether the assumption of fixed student–staff ratios, fixed real maintenance grants and the like are viable. We leave these questions until chapter 8, where we argue that there are possibilities of cost saving which will make manageable the expansion of student numbers we have suggested. We turn now to the remaining strategic question of whether the expansion is desirable on manpower grounds.

The manpower implications of expansion
There are really two issues here. From the social point of view, we want to know whether the additional graduates will be em-

ployed where their extra education makes them sufficiently more productive to warrant the cost of this extra education. From the individual point of view, it is important that higher education does not turn out to be a blind alley leading to jobs which frustrate because they do not exploit the talents developed at college.

Our projected expansion will certainly have the most profound effects on the educational composition of the adult population: the chances that the person sitting next to you on the bus will be reading the *Guardian* or *The Times* will rise sharply. In the labour force about 5 per cent, or one in twenty, have at present had full-time higher education. Suppose by 1981 we are taking 30 per cent of the age group into full-time higher education, compared with about 15 per cent now. This means that by 1981 the proportion of our labour force with higher education will have risen to 8 per cent. But the long-run effects are even more striking. Even if there were no subsequent expansion of educational opportunity, which seems most unlikely, the higher-educated proportion would by 2025 have risen to about 30 per cent of the labour force. Do we really want changes of this magnitude? There seem to be two good reasons for accepting the prospect with equanimity.

The first is the argument from the United States. In 1960 the US had a higher-educated proportion of the labour force roughly equal to ours projected for 1980. In the preceding years higher education had expanded at least as fast as our projected rate of growth. Yet there is no evidence that higher education became a less socially profitable undertaking over the period. Indeed the 'social rate of return', calculated by relating the wage differential between graduates and non-graduates to the cost of undergraduate education, was roughly constant between 1939 and 1960.[1] Thus the increased supply of graduates did not precipitate a collapse in the graduate labour market. And, even if graduates do in future become employed as foremen, who is to say that an acute mind cannot be fruitfully employed in rationalizing production at that level in the sophisticated and capital-intensive industry of the future?

A second and rather different argument springs from our belief that higher earnings are for many students a major motive

1. G. S. Becker, *Human Capital*, Princeton University Press, 1964.

for undertaking higher education. If this is so, our projections of the future demand for places in fact imply the assumption of a commensurate growth in the demand for higher-educated manpower. If the demand for manpower does not grow this fast, the demand for places will grow more slowly than in our projection. But we shall be able to see this happening and to adjust our forecast accordingly. The principle of basing provision on the demand for places will not have been vitiated.

This notion that the private demand for places will adequately reflect the economy's demand for manpower depends for precision on a number of rather stringent assumptions,[1] and also on the proposition that at present we have the right amount of manpower, given our general level of economic development. This last is a point that many would dispute, and it has become fashionable to imagine that Britain is educationally underdeveloped relative to her major competitors. As Table 7 shows, this is simply not true of science and applied science taken together. But, the critics say, in Britain it is all science and no application. This again is not true, at any rate of our current rate of output of applied scientists. As producers of professional technologists we stand marginally behind France but ahead of Germany, the Netherlands and Italy, and, if higher levels of technician training analogous to the Higher National Certificate are thrown in, we lead the (non-Communist) world. There is thus no quantitative problem; it is just that technologists have failed to penetrate the Establishment in anything like the depth achieved in other countries, and engineering has failed to attract its share of the most brilliant students. Expanding the polytechnics will not ease this – the polytechnics have in any case a different rationale. What might work would be the explicit foundation of a British MIT.[2]

If international comparisons do not persuade people that our broad supply of scientists and technologists is reasonably adequate, there is also the evidence from calculations of the social rate of return to education. These are subject to notorious

1. See R. Layard, 'Economic theories of educational planning', in M. Peston and B. Corry (eds.), *Essays in Honour of Lord Robbins*, Weidenfeld & Nicolson, 1971.

2. See the Robbins Committee's recommendations for a new Special Institute for Scientific and Technological Education and Research (Robbins, pp. 128–30).

Table 7
International Comparisons of Scientific and Technological Manpower

	S + T* graduates as % of labour force 1960–61	Numbers qualifying in S + T* as % of the age group (1964)		Numbers qualifying in T† as % of the age group (1964)	
		Graduates	Graduates + HNC level	Graduates	Graduates + HNC level
USA	1·8	4·2	4·2	1·5	1·5
UK	0·7**	2·3**	5·1	0·8*	2·9
France	0·7	2·5	3·2	1·2	1·9
Germany	0·7	0·8	2·2	0·5	2·0
Italy	0·7	0·9	0·9	0·3	0·3
Netherlands	0·4	0·8	2·6	0·4	2·0

Source: *Gaps in Technology: Analytical Report*, OECD, Paris, 1970.
*S + T indicates Science, Engineering and Technology.
†T indicates Engineering and Technology.
Levels covered are as follows:
USA All Bachelor's degrees.
UK ** Graduates: university degrees and Diploma in Technology only. If other qualified members of professional engineering institutions are included the figure of 0.7 rises to 1.0, and the graduate flow figures rise similarly.
France Graduates: universities and Grandes Ecoles. Non-graduates: 'higher technician' qualifications.
Germany Graduates: universities and *Technische Hochschulen*. Non-graduates: *Ingenieuschulen*.
Netherlands Graduates: universities and technical high schools. Non-graduates: higher technical schools and technical colleges.

problems when used as measures of the absolute position rather than of changes over time (as in our earlier discussion). But the evidence of wage levels in the electrical engineering industry does not suggest a marked shortage of scientific and engineering skills in our society. Leaving aside the psychic benefits of education and any other benefits not reflected in wages, the rate of return to undergraduate science and engineering education is about 8 per cent.[1]

But though our present position is relatively healthy, it will not remain so unless we change. Economic growth will create new professions and destroy old ones. Provided the economy expands, we need not be apprehensive about an educational expansion on the scale we have described.

1. See L. Maglen and R. Layard, 'How profitable is engineering education?', *Higher Education Review*, Spring 1970.

Chapter Three
The Present Scope and Structure of Tertiary Education

If you want to get somewhere, it is well to know where you start from. Higher education is usually defined in Britain to be that part of all education beyond school ('tertiary education') which takes its students to various points well beyond the GCE 'A' level or the ONC level. It is not identical with 'degree studies', though the higher-education sector includes the universities, which are mainly concerned with degree studies and advanced research. But the universities are not the only source of degrees, and the picture is complex in other ways as well. For instance, higher education in the technical colleges and polytechnics goes on side by side with education which is 'tertiary' but not 'higher'; and, with the arrival of the Open University, the line dividing adult education from formal degree studies is no longer clear cut. Such complications are frequently misunderstood, not only by foreign commentators, but by British ones as well – and it happens just as frequently that people in Britain make false comparisons with what happens overseas, because the differences between the systems are not appreciated. The essential features of the present structure of tertiary education in Britain are summarized by Peter Venables, who suggests some of its faults and limitations. He has necessarily painted with a broad brush; the finer points (for instance, the differences in the Scottish system) are not examined. The Open University is discussed in chapter 6 (pp. 140–44).

Peter Venables

It is against the statistical background of chapter 2, and with the long trend from the Age of Assent to the Era of Consent in mind, that we need to examine the present scale and scope of tertiary education, its merits, and the disadvantages and defects now compelling urgent attention for planning in the 1970s.

Our present institutions are the cumulative result of initiatives and innovations, and of adaptation and consolidation in response to social, economic and political factors over a long period. The present character and size of many of them are beyond the wildest hopes of their founders, and they have shown remarkable resilience and flexibility in serving the needs of successive generations, particularly in the last fifty years.[1] Over this period, the form and scope of official statistics have changed so radically (as witness the recent publications of the DES) that only very broad comparisons can be made; but these suffice for our present purposes. Tertiary education, as defined, comprises four main sectors: the universities; the colleges of education; adult education; and further education (including technical, art and commercial education). Each will be dealt with briefly in turn.[2]

The present system of tertiary education

Of the present forty-seven universities in the United Kingdom, thirty-six are in England, eight in Scotland, one in Wales and two in Northern Ireland. In 1968–9 the total number of full-time students in universities was 217,625, including 175,300 in first-degree courses and 38,415 reading for higher degrees. Of the

1. See P. Venables, 'Technical and higher education – the changing pattern', *British Association for Commercial and Industrial Education Journal*, December 1969 and January 1970.

2. For a fuller account see Venables's introduction to *Higher Education in the United Kingdom: A Handbook for Students Overseas and their Advisers*, British Council and the ACU, 1970.

total in England and Wales in 1968, there were 20,898 at Oxford and Cambridge, 31,533 at London University, 64,604 at the 'civic' universities, 14,313 at the seven 'new' universities founded 1961–5, 19,103 in the technological universities (former CATs), 13,536 in the University of Wales, 33,817 in Scotland (16,891 at Edinburgh and Glasgow) and 6,140 in Northern Ireland. There were also 21,848 on part-time courses. Of the full-time students 20·1 per cent were taking courses in arts, 20·2 in social studies, 25·9 in science, 16·0 in technology, 10·0 in medicine and associated subjects. 72·2 per cent of full-time students were men, 27·8 women, and 7·3 were from overseas.

Colleges for the training of teachers for schools were established during the nineteenth century, first by religious bodies, then from 1890 by the Board of Education, and from 1902 by the LEAs. Following the Robbins Report they became colleges of education, more closely linked with particular universities through their institutes or schools of education, and selected students became eligible to take a degree (B.Ed.) of the university. Four colleges were established especially to train technical teachers – at Bolton (1946), London (Garnett College, 1946), Huddersfield (1947) and Wolverhampton (1961). Administratively the colleges remain the responsibility of the LEAs or voluntary bodies, but recently they have gained greatly improved conditions of governance as a result of the Weaver Report.

Tertiary education comprises all education for adult citizens, but 'adult education' has traditionally been concerned with the general/liberal education of mature adults. As such it is a sector of education set apart from the usual provision in colleges and universities for students aged eighteen to the early twenties. It has a long history, stemming mainly from the Mechanics Institutes of the 1820s and from the work of religious bodies. Extra-mural adult education was begun by Cambridge in 1873 and Oxford in 1878, and courses are now provided by most universities. Voluntary bodies have contributed notably to the general development, especially the Workers' Educational Association (WEA, founded in 1903), and the residential adult education colleges. Latterly an outstanding contribution has been made by the local education authorities. Altogether the range of provision is substantial, with systematic courses of university standard sustained over several years, a diverse provision of short courses, some post-graduate refresher courses, specialist courses of all kinds, and an enormous variety of recreational classes. These are not trivial and are not to be written off as 'mere hobby classes'. Such voluntary organizations as the Townswomen's Guild, the Women's Institutes, the YMCA and the YWCA also make an invaluable contribution.

Because of the great diversity of courses and classes and of the fact that many people are involved in more than one kind of activity, it is not possible to give accurate statistics of total numbers. Suffice it to note that, in addition to the enrolments in evening institutes, in 1966–7 there were 139,963 students enrolled in university extension courses, 44,141 at adult education residential colleges, and 14,815 attending short courses; the WEA had 95,372 registered students. The body with widest concern for adult education is the National Institute of Adult Education.

In terms of full-time and part-time provision, further education is by far the largest and most diversified sector of tertiary education, with enrolments as shown in Table 8.

Table 8
Enrolments 1968–9 (in thousands)

Courses at major establishments	England and Wales	Scotland	Total
Full-time day (inc. sandwich)	243·9	20·8	264·7
Part-time day	749·7	69·9	819·6
Evening	756·6	39·3	795·9
Total at major establishments	1,750·3	130·0	1,880·2
Evening institutes	1,394·7	187·4	1,582·1

Some changes in the kind of work done have been made to overcome long-continuing defects, resulting in a greater proportion of students in day courses at major establishments of further education. Part-time day-release courses as we know them started with the National Certificate course system in 1921, and were later extended to City and Guilds Craft courses, and later still to commercial courses. These courses received a great impetus as a result of the Second World War, and more recently the Industrial Training Act of 1964. Sandwich courses were a major postwar development, designed to deal with the problem of lack of time in part-time courses by introducing full-time study, but without loss of the related industrial training. Such courses are mainly at professional and technician levels, and enrolments in Great Britain totalled 30,854 (29,606 in England and Wales) in November 1968. Evening classes, for so long the safety-valve of the educationally deprived, continued to make a significant contribution in further education. This was particularly so in the provision of 'recreational' subjects, enrolments for which account for the large majority of evening students as a whole.

Another recent important change has been the growth of advanced work in further education. Of the 1,880,000 students in further-education major establishments in Table 8, 203,000 were taking advanced courses of degree or equivalent standard, of which about 82,900 were full-time (including sandwich courses), 74,200 part-time day, and 46,300 in evening courses. Of these advanced students, 14,300 were studying for London University internal and external degrees, and 14,400 were studying for first degrees on courses (mainly sandwich) recognized by the Council for National Acadmic Awards (CNAA).

The strong links of further-education institutions with industry and commerce are important, and are exemplified by the fact that in 1968 about 709,000 employees attended day-release (including block-release) courses, and 30,900 sandwich courses. Craft and trade, and technician courses are numerous and varied, and in 1968–9 the City and Guilds of London Institute examined about 334,300 candidates in Great Britain. Under the Industrial Training Act a Central Training Council was set up to advise the Minister of Labour on general policy, and to it are to be related Industrial Training Boards for each industry. By 1970, twenty-eight of these boards had been set up, and considerable progress has been made in the immense task of devising and approving schemes of training for industries covering a total working population of some fifteen million. In the year ending March

1968 the boards expended a levy totalling over £120 million. The scale and nature of these developments are closely affecting the work of technical colleges, especially at craft and technician level, while the universities and polytechnics are becoming increasingly involved at professional level and in education and training for management.

The expansion of tertiary education required by 1980 must affect substantially, if not radically, both its range and structure. Proposals to cope with these future needs, however, cannot proceed without regard to the nature of existing institutions. In particular, the size and complexity of further education requires a brief description of its structure, and how it came into being, before any proposals can be usefully discussed. This is essential to an understanding of the 'binary system' policy described by the Secretary of State Anthony Crosland in March 1965, and in considering how far and in what ways it should be modified over the next decade.

Further-education institutions have grown variously in response to local, regional and national needs, and not as part of a planned system of tertiary education – the Robbins Report refused to describe the result as a system at all. The Ministry of Education pamphlet *Further Education* (1946) envisaged new roles for county colleges, local colleges of further education and regional colleges, but firm planning did not become official policy until after the White Paper on Technical Education (1956). The basic structure is shown in Table 9. The table oversimplifies by omitting specific reference to separate colleges of art, colleges of commerce, national colleges and their varied relationships with technical colleges, a number of which themselves contained schools of art and departments of commerce and, in a few cases, a national college as well. Teacher-training colleges were not part of this sector of further education, and never regarded themselves as such – because, as we have seen, so many were independent foundations aided in varying degrees by LEAs, and because, as a result of the McNair Report, *Teachers and Youth Leaders* (1944), they had become linked with the universities through 'institutes of education'.

The colleges of advanced technology, especially, had made remarkable progress by 1963, partly because of the clarification of policy and the commitment to increased resources following the 1956 White Paper, and partly because of the inception of the Diploma of Technology under the National Council for Technological Awards (NCTA), established by the government in July 1955. This seven-year period was a highly formative one, almost as if the Robbins Report had shed its illumination before the event of its publication in 1963. Such committees and commissions, however, arise from a ferment of dissatisfactions and discussions that can no longer be ignored, and official recognition when it comes is often a confirmation of trends already under way. One significant straw in the wind of change was the transfer in 1962 of those colleges of advanced technology still under the administration of the LEAs to independent status under trust deeds, and financed by direct grant from the Ministry.

The structure shown in Table 9 has undergone two major changes since 1963. First of all, the four-tier structure was truncated when the colleges of advanced technology were granted charters as independent technological universities in 1966–7: Loughborough; Aston in Birmingham; the City University in London (formerly Northampton College/Polytechnic); Brunel at Uxbridge; Bath (formerly Bristol College); Bradford; Surrey (formerly Battersea College/Polytechnic); and Salford. In 1967 the Welsh College was incorporated within the University of Wales as the Institute of Science and Technology, and the Chelsea College became the Chelsea College of Science and Technology within the University of London. In addition to these changes, the Manchester College of Technology was incorporated within Manchester University, and is known as the University of Manchester Institute of Science and Technology. In Scotland the Royal Technical College, Glasgow, gained its charter as the University of Strathclyde in 1964, and the Heriot-Watt College, Edinburgh, its charter as a university in 1966.

The second major modification is the result of the announcement in May 1966 of the Government's intention to organize polytechnics as the apex of the non-university system, from among the regional colleges shown in the diagram and certain colleges of art and commerce. The policy is that polytechnics are to be mainly teaching institutions, though with some research, and that they will be closely linked with industry and

Table 9
Structure of Technical Education at the Time of Publication of the Robbins Committee Report (October 1963)

Qualifications		Number	Likely future number	Types of courses	Courses for
Dip. Tech., B.Sc. London; professional qualifications; postgraduate diplomas; higher degrees and diplomas	Colleges of advanced technology	10 ⟶ ?		PT + FT	University level only TGT + P + research + postgraduate
Some Dip. Tech. and B.Sc. London; professional qualifications; Higher National Diplomas and Certificates; City and Guilds Final examination	Regional colleges	25 ⟶ 30?		PT + FT	Superior TN + C + some TGT + P + some postgraduate and research
Some Higher and Ordinary National Certificates; some City and Guilds Final and Inter examinations; general education, e.g. GCE 'O' and 'A' level; domestic and catering courses*	Area colleges	155† ⟶ 210†		PT + FT	TN + C + some P

Ordinary National Certificates; City and Guilds Inter and some Final examinations; general education, e.g. GCE 'O' level and some 'A' level; full-time domestic, catering courses, etc.*	Local colleges of further education	275?† ⟶ ?†	PT + FT	TN + C + general education
*Commercial courses not indicated, though many technical colleges have commerce departments and courses; the same is true for art courses and schools within technical colleges	Four-tier structure — see White Paper on Technical Education (Cmd 9703) and Ministry of Education Circular 305	†No official numbers yet stated	PT = part-time courses FT = full-time courses, including sandwich courses	TGT = technologists TN = technicians C = craftsmen P = courses to graduateship of professional institutions

Colleges of advanced technology Battersea (London); Birmingham; Bradford; Bristol; Brunel (Middlesex); Chelsea (London); Loughborough; Northampton (London); Salford; Welsh (Cardiff)

Regional colleges Borough (London); Brighton; Brixton (London); Hatfield College of Technology; Huddersfield; Kingston-upon-Thames; Lanchester College of Technology, Coventry; Leeds College of Technology; Leicester; Liverpool (Building); Liverpool (Technology); North Staffordshire; Northern (London); Nottingham; Plymouth and Devonport; Portsmouth; Rugby; Rutherford College of Technology (Newcastle-upon-Tyne); Sir John Cass (London); South-East Essex Technical College, School of Art (Dagenham); Sunderland; The Polytechnic (London); Treforest; West Ham; Woolwich (London) commerce. For present purposes they are simply listed for comparison with Table 9; their functions and future are discussed later in this chapter, and also in chapter 6.

Of the thirty proposed polytechnics listed below, twenty-six had been formally designated by 1 September 1969:

Birmingham; Bristol; Glamorgan (Treforest); Hatfield; Huddersfield; Lanchester (Coventry and Rugby); Leeds; Leicester; Liverpool; Manchester; Middlesbrough; Teeside; Newcastle upon Tyne; North Staffordshire (Stafford and Stoke); Nottingham; Oxford; Plymouth; Portsmouth; Preston; Sheffield; Sunderland; Wolverhampton. Greater London, the following groupings: Northern Polytechnic and Northwestern Polytechnic; Borough Polytechnic, Brixton School of Building, National College of Heating and Ventilating, Refrigeration and Farm Engineering, and City of Westminster College; City of London College, Nautical College, and Sir John Cass College; The Polytechnic Regent Street, and the Holborn College of Law, Languages and Commerce; Woolwich Polytechnic and the Hammersmith College of Art and Building; Barking College of Technology, West Ham College of Technology, and the South-West Essex Technical College and School of Art; Kingston (Kingston upon Thames); Hendon College of Technology, Enfield College of Technology and Hornsey College of Art.

Discussions began in September 1970 about the establishment of a polytechnic based on the Harris Institute, Preston. In November 1969 the existing and proposed polytechnics had some 68,000 students in full-time and sandwich courses, 65,000 in part-time day courses, and about 39,000 in evening-only courses. Nearly 20,000 students were taking courses for CNAA degrees in November 1969, and most of these were students at the polytechnics. Courses in the polytechnics will lead mainly to the award of degrees by the CNAA, whereas two other institutions in the further-education sector have been granted charters with the power to grant their own degrees. These are the Royal College of Art in 1967, and the College of Aeronautics at Cranfield as the Cranfield Institute of Technology as from November 1969. These two are in receipt of direct grant from the DES, whereas the polytechnics remain under the LEAs. A third institution in receipt of direct grant from the DES, but not administratively under the LEAs nor related to the UGC, is the Open University, which was granted its charter in May 1969, and which teaches through television, correspondence courses and local groups. In their respective ways, the foregoing three institutions constitute important departures from tradition, and may prove valuable precedents for securing greater flexibility in future developments.

This then is, all too briefly perhaps, a summary outline of the four main sectors of tertiary education, and of the complexities of the further-education sector in particular. The government's 'binary policy' for higher and further education is discussed later (chapters 5, 6 and 7).

Limits to educational opportunity

Certain other aspects must be discussed as part of the general background; some of them are adverse social factors, others are delays in development now embedded in the system, and yet others are manifest defects in tertiary education : some are inter-related, and the general cumulative effect is one of limiting educational opportunity. They are not difficult to determine, and are listed under seven heads.

1. The proportion of the age groups aged eighteen, nineteen and twenty inclusive, in full-time tertiary education (including sandwich courses) is too low to meet the aspirations of qualified candidates, and future social and economic needs (chapter 2).

2. The proportion of the age groups attending part-time day-release courses is too small. Day release grew haphazardly over the decades, and proved to be an arduous system, with very sub-stantial wastage figures which were publicized in the Crowther Report. While the total numbers have increased substantially over the years, despite all the difficulties, the *proportion* of the age groups in attendance has not risen substantially, as is shown in Table 10.

The levelling-off of the curve of expansion, despite the work of the industrial training boards, reflects many limiting factors, including the apathy of employers – especially in smaller firms – and the fact that employers who are forced to pay the levy can-not legally be required to release their employees. Any reform of tertiary education which fails to deal with such factors will in-evitably be limited, if not stultified. But the case for reform goes

Table 10

Increase in Day Release in England and Wales, 1951–1958–1968

Age group	November 1951		November 1958		November 1968	
	Numbers in part-time day release (000's)	% of relevant age group in population	Numbers in part-time day release (000's)	% of relevant age group in population	Numbers in part-time day release (000's)	% of relevant age group in population
15 to 17	145·7	8·7	181·7	10·3	254·6	12·9
18 to 20	75·8	4·5	144·8	8·5	244·5	11·3

further than that, once it is realized that release for one day a week (a provision which stems from the Fisher Act of 1919) cannot, even if extended and secured, be adequate to the needs of the 1970s and 1980s. The increase of time required for study and acquiring skills at all levels (but without loss of essential industrial training) is so substantial as to require a total change to a different system, i.e. to substantial block release and sandwich courses.

3. Part-time day-release courses show most clearly the inequality of educational opportunities for women, as Table 11, based on a comparison with Table 10, reveals. Moreover, proportionately compared with men, there has been no improvement over the last decade.

Table 11

Part-Time Day Release of Women from Employment in England and Wales, 1951–1958–1968

Age group	November 1951		November 1958		November 1968	
	Numbers in part-time day release (000's)	% of relevant age group in population	Numbers in part-time day release (000's)	% of relevant age group in population	Numbers in part-time day release (000's)	% of relevant age group in population
15 to 17	28·8	3·5	38·3	4·4	52·6	5·4
18 to 20	7·4	0·9	12·7	1·5	22·9	2·1

The proportion of the eighteen- to twenty-year-old population who were in full-time courses (including sandwich) in further-education establishments was, in 1968, for women 2·5 per cent, and for men 4·9; in the universities the proportions were 2·7 per cent for women, 5·9 for men. The figures reflect many attitudes (p. 13), but also the close link between occupations and educational opportunity: as, for example, between male-dominated occupations, and those in which women are largely employed which are less rewarding or casual. This is reinforced by the strong vocational orientation and content of day-release courses, and the fact that general education is not seen to be sufficient justification for day release – as witness the much lower rate of release for those employed in commerce and service industries.

4. The inequitable geographical distribution of educational opportunity has been the subject of a number of recent surveys, showing the greater provision of sixth forms and of university places south of a line from the Wash to the Bristol Channel. With the strong 'tech' traditions of the north, it would be surprising if this imbalance was not reversed for further education, because of its preponderant part-time provision for the educationally deprived.

5. Social conditions, especially levels and conditions of employment, markedly influence educational opportunity, as the Robbins Report clearly demonstrated. The effects are cumulatively negative, and the unawareness, the lack of knowledge, and perhaps the lack of sympathy on the part of employers and parents are obstacles against which progress has to be made. This is indeed a powerful argument for the provision of adult education alongside other forms of education. Educationally and in other ways, second-generation graduates thus have a better start in life than first-generation ones, still more than those who have graduated or taken HNC 'the hard way', while those without such education and training – in fact the great majority – are most disadvantaged.

6. Most large systems have their own momentum and inherent inflexibility, and educational systems are no exception. The increased rate of change in the structure of employment, the modification, even transformation, of long-established industries and occupations, the obsolescence of some, and the unpredictable emergence of entirely new ones, make it increasingly difficult to plan first-degree and diploma courses precisely for them. The inflexibility is shown in two main ways: the time-lag in changing the content of courses to meet new needs, with consequential

changes in teaching methods; and the lack of adequate provision at a later stage for the specialist subjects (appropriately modified) which have been deferred in order to make room for more basic subjects, especially science.

7. The lack of flexibility is not only evident internally within institutions, but also in the lack of a designed relatedness to each other. Again this is shown in two main ways: in the location and design of courses, and the lack of opportunity for students to take subjects in other institutions as options in their main courses in their own institutions; and likewise in the lack of systems of 'credit', which would enable a student to transfer from one institution to another at particular stages. These are increasingly important because of the growing specialization of tertiary institutions, partly in order to conserve, indeed maximize, the combined use of costly equipment (e.g. computers and nuclear research plant) and highly specialized staffing, and partly in response to regional needs (as with textiles and ceramics). The most important consideration is to facilitate the flow of ability to and through particular courses and institutions to the maximum advantage.

These seven aspects need especially to be borne in mind in considering the prospects for future change set out in later chapters.

Chapter Four
Three Essays on the Nature of Higher Education in a Decade of Expansion

If provision for full-time higher education needs to be about doubled by 1981 (as suggested in chapter 2) where are the students to go? The possibilities are the universities (either the present system, or one enlarged by new institutions or the conversion to universities of other sorts of institutions); the polytechnics; the colleges of education, with enlarged functions; the rest of the further-education system; new kinds of institution, such as junior colleges and liberal-arts colleges; and the Open University. It seems unlikely that differences in cost will be decisive in determining policy – nor should they be, for the first priority should be the definition of the objectives and purposes of different kinds of institution, and an examination of the principles which should determine the distribution of students, of which the attainment of low cost is only one among many. The Robbins Report could fairly be criticized as having said very little on what higher education is, or ought to be, about. In this chapter George Brosan outlines a philosophy for the newest type of institution, the polytechnic; Charles Carter discusses the seven activities which (in varying proportions) go on in institutions of higher education, and the variety which is needed if higher education is to develop the whole civilized man; and Peter Venables proposes seven principles which should govern expansion in higher (and in tertiary) education. Our hope is that these different manners of approach will, by their interaction, stimulate thinking on the difficult and fundamental issues. Without such thinking, higher education will drift, and become increasingly unrelated to the real needs of the community.

George Brosan
A Polytechnic Philosophy

Social dynamics is a phrase used by Thurman Arnold to describe the behaviour of social institutions, i.e. a set of rationalized, conscious organizations that perform society's functions. Money, joint stock companies, religion and education are examples of institutions. These institutions have creeds, i.e. sets of beliefs which may – or may not – be explicitly enunciated. The creed of the universities is dealt with in chapter 6.

There is another creed in the institution of education, which, put simply, is that people should be trained to do jobs. This crude vocational need first made itself manifest on a significant scale during the first industrial revolution, and as a consequence the institution of education split into two parts: the universities did not absorb the need to train mechanics, plumbers and so on; they were dealt with separately in their mechanics' institutes. This is the first example of one of the laws of social dynamics, which states that where there is acute conflict between the ideals and the practical needs of an institution – in this case the institution of education – the institution will split into two parts. One will represent the ideal, and the other will cater for the practical activity which contradicts the ideal. Over the years the social need for educating people has gradually become more respectable; the aristocratic prejudice against education both declined and was seen to be dysfunctional. It was quite predictable that the organization representing the ideal, i.e. the universities, would have a higher place in the social hierarchy than the organization doing the practical job.

The reason for this can be understood as follows. A social need appears to be fulfilled. When an existing organization fails to carry out a needed task, an undercover or immoral organization emerges. The ideal – in this case the universities – is represented by a highly moral organization and holds the view that the social need is not real need at all but a form of sin. Why should all these people have any form of education? What are we educating them for? Are we not making them more miserable by arousing expectations that cannot be fulfilled? And so on. The mechanics' institutes, technical colleges and polytechnics which successively recognized the need and dealt with it represent a 'bastard' organization, i.e. an organization which is not socially acceptable. These bastard organizations have to be tolerated as a type of necessary evil, e.g. in the same way as the Church accepts the existence of the Devil. As in many other cases where the need is not recognized as legitimate, the organization catering to the ideal philosophy – the pursuit of knowledge – is considered to be respectable, and the organization carrying out the job, i.e. fulfilling the need, is regarded as non-respectable. Hence the colleges of technology, and now the polytechnics – which deal at university level with the vocational needs of society – have hitherto been non-respectable.

In some senses the two organizations give public battle with each other. The respectable organization tries to satisfy the ideal by attempting to swallow up the non-respectable one, but despite this the non-respectable one must survive. It will do so because it is indeed fulfilling a need, and because the scrutiny that the struggle produces will inevitably make it adopt an efficient and disciplined organization. This is what has in fact happened in the struggle between the autonomous and public sectors of higher education.

In the early autumn of 1967 the Vice-Chancellor of Liverpool University at that time gave a highly condescending speech. He referred to work in polytechnics-to-be by the use of phrases such as 'cheaper way of getting degrees', and went on to say that polytechnics would produce 'second-class citizens in the graduate world'. The inference was that while the polytechnics would provide higher education, the universities would provide 'real' education. This deliberate cultivation of ill-founded antagonism can perhaps be excused on the grounds of lack of knowledge at the time.

The attempted suppression of the bastard organization takes the form described in the Robbins Report, as well as elsewhere; to expand the traditional universities – so that technical colleges doing work at university level will become unnecessary – and to give the name of university to some institutions which can no longer be suppressed, such as the former colleges of advanced technology. This accelerated the trend in many colleges of advanced technology to pattern themselves on existing universities with the same attitudes of staff and students. The trends were due to the difference in status, and to the social and monetary privileges attached to higher status.

The ideas held by the organizations representing the ideal inhibit their action in many ways. A university would not consider training television mechanics, although clearly there is a need for television mechanics to be trained. There is yet another law of social dynamics that says that the gradual decline and fall of social institutions is not the result of the antagonistic ideas held by their opponents, but rather the product of the inhibitions against practical action resulting from their institutional creeds. Changes are often described as being due to new ideas, and so they probably are. But an alternative analysis is that the failure of some organization to act will leave a social gap into which some new organization will flow. A comparison of the English and Scottish systems is illuminating in this respect.

In England, the technical-college system is relatively strong, as a result of the attitudes and inaction of the English universities. In Scotland, by comparison, the technical-college system is relatively weak, because of the greater amount of action and broader base of the Scottish universities.

If Oxford and Cambridge had been involved with their own communities, neither Oxford Polytechnic nor the Cambridge College of Technology would have existed. On the other hand, it is inevitable that a social need which is not in accord with the ideal part of the creed will not be met competently until it evolves a philosophy of its own. The process of building up a philosophy from which a policy and a practical programme can be derived is, in any society, at least troublesome and irksome, and may well be physically or intellectually violent. Were it possible for an objective view to be taken the need would not arise. In Africa some people actually starve because their particular tribe has a philosophy which precludes the eating of fish; tons of available protein in fish catches are neglected by semi-starving men and women. In Great Britain there is currently no philosophy which allows for mass higher education, let alone universal higher education. Nor shall I here advocate one; there is a more urgent task. It is to outline, however broadly, a philosophy for polytechnics.

Matching or monitoring

The starting-point is economic survival. In a general sense there are significant links between education and economic change. Education is concerned with all that mankind does and all that mankind does adds to or subtracts from economic progress. Education has its effects on population growth, on health and hence the vigour of the community, on rises and falls in demands for various goods and services – including that of education itself.

What are the consequent implications, for the work of colleges, of the expectations of the economy and of society in general? That there is such a link is undeniable; that its form and relevance are more difficult to define is also abundantly clear. Consider, for example, two conflicting research reports on the value of education to economic growth. The first, carried out by Mabel Newcomer,[1] showed that there were fewer graduates in fast-growing companies than in slowly growing ones. By far the greater proportion of graduates were in the latter. This led to the tentative conclusion that education of these executives tended to reduce their ability to contribute to economic growth by entrepreneurial effort. On the other hand, the second piece of research (by Harbison and Myers[2]) was able to show significant positive correlation between a composite index of 'human resources', based mainly on educational criteria and GNP per capita, for no less than seventy-five countries at various growth-levels. Again, consider the contradiction about education on one hand in the report of the Brookings Institution on the UK economy,[3] and the views of Enoch Powell on the other. In the simplest terms, the Brookings Institution says that the UK has quite in-

1. *The Big Business Executive*, Columbia University Press, 1965.
2. *Management in the Industrial World*, McGraw-Hill, 1959, and *Education, Manpower and Economic Growth*, McGraw-Hill, 1969.
3. Richard E. Caves and Associates, *Britain's Economic Prospects*, Allen & Unwin, 1968.

adequate higher education, while Enoch Powell says we have too much. Assuming that neither view is malevolently motivated, what are we to make of the situation? Part of the difficulty arises from the various functions of the social institution of education. There is the view of education as a desirable object of consumption by students, and the view of education as an investment in (human) resources by the community. There is also another distinction, that of *matching* and *monitoring*, which needs consideration. To do so we use a 'model' of society. Such a model must, of course, be grossly simplified and cannot allow for all the possible interactions that really occur.

It is regrettably true that there are no good grounds for assuming a *simple* relation between education and economic growth. If planning is taken as a whole, no theoretical method currently exists which enables us to decide whether economic targets should be fixed and educational development adapted to them, or vice-versa. The most that can be said is that the two are inter-related. Suppose we ask: What resources shall be allocated to education? The 'bunkum' theory proposed by Enoch Powell[1] gives one answer, but other views and methods need to be considered. The classical return-on-investment method is not very functional in this case, mainly because there is not sufficient data to enable decisions to be made on how to allocate funds to high-rate-of-return sectors. That is, there is no theoretical method currently available which tells us how to distribute money to best advantage as between different types of education, or between teachers, buildings, equipment, libraries, etc. in each type.

One approach which does yield some useful information is based on manpower planning.[2] It uses the socio-economic model proposed by the Battelle Memorial Institute. The model, shown in outline in Figure 2, was developed to deal with simultaneous changes in society. For example, a change may be characterized by a new product; it will cause new demands and cause competition among products. More important in the present context is the fact that technological changes in the processes used

1. 'The growth theory of education is bunkum', speech in London, 22 June 1968.

2. But see comment by Richard Layard and Gareth Williams (p. 76).

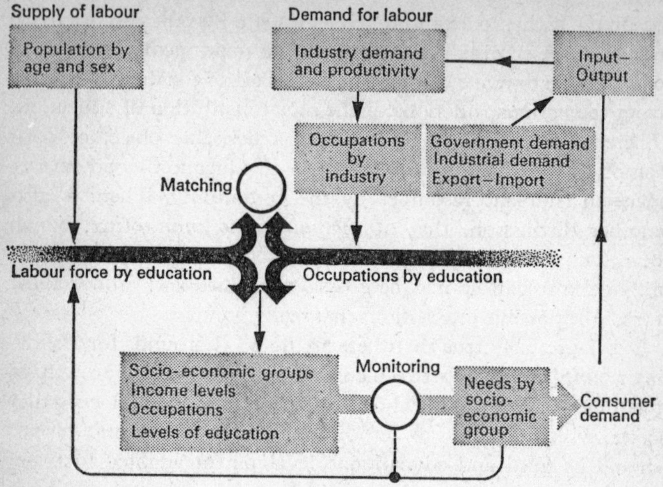

Figure 2 A modified version of the Batelle socio-economic model

in manufacture, distribution, marketing, etc. of new products and new services result in changes in skills required in the labour force. And as these processes require skill change, the components of education and training offered to the labour force by the first component of the educational system must also change.

This is the matching function of education, to *minimize the differences* between the education and training required by industry, commerce, etc., and the education, skills and knowledge that people have. The model provides a basis for analysis both of economic structures now existing and those proposed for the future. It is able, albeit in an approximate way, to relate the supply of labour to the demand for labour in various industries. Despite the somewhat primitive state of the art, types of employment required in each industrial sector can be approximated to deduce the education and training required by people employed in that sector. By doing this over the whole work force, rather on the lines of the manpower studies of the Department of Employment, a first estimate of overall educational demands can be made. From this, it is possible to work out the needs for educational activities in the future, and hence the resources for carrying out these activities.

These are not mere theories; the model has been used, for example, with considerable success in Michigan, and has enabled that state to 'provide an excellent framework for evaluating the relations between changing occupational structure and the associated requirements of the educational system. . . .' The relation assumed between economic growth and education has – at least in this one case – been shown to work. The idea of matching is several stages beyond a crude vocationalism in both conceptual content and in logistic detail. To deal with the latter, as less important, first; the idea of matching is not in any sense meant as fitting people into holes. Matching does not presume to tell individuals what to do, far less imply crudely restricted training for one or more of the areas of activity. Teaching the application of knowledge should not be thought of as determined only by the needs of industry; it is equally matching the needs of individual students. As another example, it would be very questionable whether in the UK there should be a massive investment to expand schools or departments dealing with underground mining. An increase in investment in industries and activities which are likely to be expanding by 1980 is however justifiable both morally and economically; morally, because people ultimately have to work for a living or be supported by others; economically, because of the further growth it will promote.

In conceptual content, matching should not be identified with training people for dead-end jobs today. Indeed, such simplistic vocational statements are a parody of what is required. To carry out a function effectively in 1980 will require education today which is oriented to change, since there is no means of telling what the problems of 1980 will be. It will require an ability to identify situations and abstract problems from these situations; the problems themselves may (or most likely may not) be identified with normal disciplines of the conventional curriculum. They will have components which are supra-technological and (in

1980) will include, for example, components which are sociological, economic and aesthetic.

It is no use in a matching education teaching only concepts; the ability to recognize and evaluate counter-concepts must be as effectively inculcated. Thus in business education, it is no use simply teaching students to deal with marketing within the present social structure; students must be introduced to the ideas of what might be the equivalent function of marketing in a completely different social structure. Marketing *par excellence* implies sensitivity to social change, of course; but so do many other areas of operation. They should not be predicated on the assumption of an invariant socio-economic structure.

The key features of matching education are therefore:

1. To enable students to acquire new approaches so that in future situations in which they find themselves they will be able to define and solve problems in a broad context (social, economic, technical, etc.).

2. To enable present and future students to develop their own answers to the question 'In which direction shall we go?' Opportunities – and at the crunch, capital resources – are matched to the likely development of all activities, not only the growth of manufacturing industry. There is, therefore, a large difference between matching education, and narrow training for some single and specific industrial function.

There is, however, another task which education needs to carry out, apart from the matching function. It has traditionally been carried out by the universities. While the term 'universities' does not refer to a monolithic organization, there is nevertheless substantial support within them for corporate freedom, that is, the ability to decide autonomously on the purposes of the university institution and apply resources accordingly. It is quite correct that the values of the university should be defended against all comers, including the holders of the public purse. The reason is that *any* activity in society is worthy of some comment: there needs to be an agency in society which is able by virtue of its independence to consider all activities and comment on them freely. It has been carried out for many centuries by universities. This function of observation and free comment uninfluenced directly by the executants of the events is a feedback function, a function which reveals the results of activities so that future activities can be modified. I call it *monitoring*, by analogy with the term in system theory. It is characteristic of highly active systems that if there is no feedback or monitoring, or if the feedback and monitoring are inadequate either in quantity or quality, the main activity itself may become unstable. This has happened often enough with the social system. Examples of transient activities amounting to a form of mass hysteria, e.g. the South Sea Bubble, are plentiful. The rush towards economic expansion in the USA in 1945 produced growth; the present instabilities in that country may well be a result of action on which there was little effective comment. The US universities have on the whole been involved in and not independent of the economic growth, both financially and ethically. A similar situation can be detected in Japan.

It is, therefore, absolutely essential that there shall be a social agency which is able to comment on society without looking over its shoulder. There is the strongest possible presumption in favour of allowing universities, individually as well as collectively, the greatest possible independence. And in so far as universities need to be independent of society to discharge their monitoring function, there is indeed an important sense in which universities ought quite properly to be citadels of privilege.

As will be seen from Figure 2, the monitoring function is such that it affects the intrinsic demand of the labour force on itself – what education people think they *ought* to have. It also affects the other perceived needs of the various socio-economic groups, changes (albeit slow), consumer demand, and so on.

The major confusions that arise in discussions on the relationship of education to society and the economy are due to a failure to distinguish between the matching and monitoring functions.

Take first the famous, or infamous, speech by Enoch Powell on the sacred cows of education. Clearly Powell is right if one interprets his remarks as applying to the monitoring system. Over-expansion in the monitoring section will not necessarily lead to any growth at all, and may indeed do just the opposite by the creation of an unemployed and unemployable intellectual class. Clearly, also, the Brookings Institution report (and other reports, e.g. by OECD) are right if their remarks are interpreted as applying to the matching section. One remark from the Brookings Report is worth paraphrasing. This is to the effect that the worst sort of damage any country can inflict on itself is to prevent its citizens getting the education they need, demand and are ready for. That is, the matching section must produce a match. But to do this, it requires money.

From Figure 2 we can also make a preliminary distinction between the differing roles of the colleges and the universities. The main task of the system of higher education outside the universities is to deal with the matching section, i.e. to provide a basis of manpower that the universities have *not* provided. The main task of the universities is to monitor, and the values appropriate to this task have been stated. They are also values that should under no circumstances whatever be adopted in polytechnics. They are, in any event, quite inappropriate in colleges dealing with craft and technician work, and to adopt them in the polytechnics (because the polytechnics also deal with degrees) would be a betrayal, not only of the universities, but of the polytechnics. For, if the binary system is to have any meaning, then above all the polytechnics need a philosophy of action from which a working policy and an effective programme can be derived. Such a philosophy cannot be formulated by imitating existing universities, despite Chesterton's admonition that if a thing is worth doing at all then it is worth doing badly.

The vital task of the matching section of higher education in general and the polytechnics in particular is to cause knowledge to be applied. This determines their educational characteristics, which are different from, but not inherently inferior to, those of the universities. The distinction between matching and monitoring functions helps one to understand several other dissonances. The monitoring or knowledge-seeking philosophy is not very functional when considering a policy for action in educating, say, mechanical engineers. As a specific example, the creative design required of mechanical engineers has been badly neglected in favour of the idea that mechanical engineering is concerned with doing more abstract problems, i.e. hard sums about mechanical devices. Similarly, the matching philosophy has produced no significant contribution when dealing with growth of ideas in monitoring functions, e.g. literary criticism. Again, the sweeping changes and radical reconstructions required by various reports issued on British higher education cannot be made maximally effective unless the distinct roles are recognized and preserved. Suspicion must be allayed that the Labour government elected in 1966, or any other, was pursuing an educational policy that was crudely utilitarian and spitefully egalitarian, and using the avowed needs of the matching section to scold and harass the older universities. Suspicion must be allayed that the efforts of the matching section are not based on reputable and reliable forecasts, but on transient snapshots of industrial need. Finally, the interaction between the two functions must be recognized and clarified; that is, the monitoring section has needs which are supplied by the economy; and at the same time the monitoring section functions to modify the economy. The matching section supplies one essential component in the future economy and has needs (feedback) supplied directly by the monitoring section. The fact that the philosophies and functions are different does not make them any less dependent on each other.

The response to the matching section must of course include provision of education at all higher-education levels, not only at degree level; it must deal with re-training (which is associated with redundancy, actual or threatened) and with updating, which is based on the simple premise that a single training is not enough for a lifetime of work.

What is the polytechnic philosophy?

The concept of service to society, which I have taken as a leading feature of the philosophy of polytechnics, needs a good deal of refining. In the modern world education has become the means for achieving social mobility and economic advantage. Its possessor can overcome disadvantages of inherited position and inherited wealth (or the lack of it). In real terms, performance in higher education increasingly determines future life-style, career, and sometimes even overall opportunity. There are of course notable exceptions to this as to every other general statement. And yet to develop individual students' potential for growth or communal productivity or wealth does not mean that the polytechnic is not serving intellectual ends.

A historical study will show that the transformation of the medieval university which took place after the early Renaissance had the effect of making the acquisition of knowledge moderately respectable. The process has of course developed greatly, and currently it is accepted without question that all knowledge is useful, and that its acquisition is a worthwhile activity for a reasonable man. I am not saying here that its acquisition is not reasonable but that its acquisition is currently respectable; one of King John's robber barons (or his serfs for that matter) would likely have taken a very different view.

In just the same way as the universities have made the acquisition of knowledge respectable, so the polytechnics have the task of making the *application* of knowledge respectable. This is a very different task. It does not decry the function of the universities in the generation and transmission of knowledge, but goes a step further and is concerned with the way in which this knowledge is to be used. In part, in doing so, it begins (however inadequately) to meet the students' views on the lack of correlation between degree studies and everyday life – a view usually incompletely and inaccurately expressed as a need for 'relevance'.

The idea of making the application of knowledge the central theme of the polytechnic philosophy enables other ideas to be considered. If students are to be encouraged to learn how to apply their knowledge, they will do so as individuals; the polytechnics therefore serve not some abstract concept such as Society, but the needs of each individual student. Again, the inculcation of the application of knowledge is a sharply different thing from skill training; the application of a skill may only require a little knowledge (although it can often be improved by knowing more). Application of knowledge cannot take place in a vacuum; it must be applied in a real situation in which other people are involved. To communicate with, and conclude mutually agreeable transactions with other people requires much more than a psychologically simplistic technical training, no matter how technically sophisticated the latter may be. It requires a broad understanding of the behaviour of people, of moral, ethical and social patterns which – as far as we know – give a good indication of the way people behave. It requires a student to mature in a real-world context and not in one limited to considerations of intellect. This is what the polytechnics mean when they say that the education they are interested in is vocational, although I readily concede that it is an extension of the normal usage of 'vocational'. There seems however to be no other suitable term available. Perhaps 'life-enhancing' is the nearest.

One most important consequence that results, if we take the central theme of polytechnics to be the application of knowledge, is the emergence of the idea of initiative. I believe that we are not put into this world merely to sit still and know; we are put into the world to act. The philosophical orientation of much prior education has been to avoid emphasizing initiative, at least in terms of action. By re-emphasizing the application of knowledge, polytechnics can to a very considerable extent answer many current industrial comments on the attitudes, as distinct from the knowledge, of students entering work. This is a complex topic, but a good deal of work is being done on the communication of action (coupling) as distinct from the communication of facts.

The final consequence of the application-of-knowledge theme that is relevant at the moment is the time-span. The conventional cry against education that can be applied is that it is useful for too short a time. If all that is taught and learned in a course is that which is immediately useful, the criticism is valid. But the idea of teaching and learning how to apply knowledge is a very different thing; it means that the student must be able in future years to apply any further knowledge that he acquires. And with the rate of expansion of knowledge, he will certainly acquire some! He will acquire it not necessarily for its own sake, but *in order to use it*. This is a lifetime facility, not a transient virtue.

One dilemma which the polytechnics face in completing a philosophical positive is the problem of what I will call the 'non-technologies'. On the one hand, the more classically oriented academics may infer that polytechnics are merely technologically oriented; they are thought of and referred to as 'banausic' (workshop-like) places dealing with a restricted range of 'subject material' which is mostly connected with the processes of engineering. On the other hand there is a large, although perhaps diminishing, number of industrial folk who view the introduction of any studies other than advanced skill training into what was once the local mechanics' institute as a perversion of public funds and intelligent effort. Both views are, as stated here, extreme, and in truth are rarely enunciated as plainly; but the underlying thoughts persist. They can be refuted not by other thoughts but by facts. From their inception polytechnics have made it clear that they will be concerned with a wide range of studies; even the plan for setting them up made this explicit. The width extends over all major branches of study other than medicine. Of course engineering exists, but so do subjects ranging from architecture to zoology. My own establishment, the North-East London Polytechnic, has seven faculties which I normally list as follows: Science, Engineering, Environmental Studies, Human Sciences, Business, Arts, and Art and Design. A broadly similar pattern applies to most of the bigger polytechnics, and I know of no polytechnic, whatever its size, which is concerned only with a narrow range of technological studies.

The width of study at a polytechnic is great; apart from the above incomplete list of broad areas, there are a whole host of specialities. But studies available at a polytechnic have an added feature, in that they offer a wide range of work of variable depth. That is, they offer courses in (say) Business Studies, not only at first- and second-degree level, but also at sub-degree level, that is as a Higher National Diploma in Business Studies; as part-time degree work; as part-time sub-degree work; and as part of a very wide range of professional qualifications. This is trite and obvious; on an accelerating scale the qualifications are beginning to be related to each other, so that movement between the courses is not only possible, but is actually happening. Because the studies are held in the same place, part-time students following a Higher National Certificate (HNC) course interact with full-time students on a degree course, for example in seminars. The result is of immense value to both. It is this kind of breadth, apart from the breadth of subject-matter, that enables polytechnics to view comments about lack of breadth with at least puzzlement, if not actual disdain.

A seminar in which a business-degree student talks at length with a junior manager of a transport firm will probably teach both more in terms of human interaction and moral development than any amount of purely intellectual discussion.[1] In such practical ways, it seems that we are beginning to see the end of teaching in a purely syntactical mode remote from the immediacy of sense data and personal experiences. I think that we are almost ready to embark on a re-styling of curricula which involve the elements of life that are personal, real and expressive, rather than merely intellectual.

1. I am indebted to Alan Hale for organizing such seminars at Enfield College.

*Richard Layard and
Gareth Williams*

A Comment on Manpower Forecasting

As people who have both been involved in manpower-forecasting exercises of the kind discussed by George Brosan in the last chapter,[1] we feel that he is far too sanguine about the possible uses of this kind of exercise in the existing state of knowledge, especially in the leading industrial countries of the world. The problem is twofold. First it is difficult to establish what is the optimal manpower structure even at the present. For example, there is wide disagreement about whether we have now too many or too few engineers; and, though rate of return analysis and job analysis can help, there is no clear-cut answer. Second, there are the uncertainties about future changes in the optimal structure, which depend on changes in industrial structure and in the technology of each industry, and on the implications of these for the manpower structure. There are some useful things which can be said here, and it is certainly better to try to give them quantitative rather than qualitative expression. But too much accuracy should not be looked for.

In short, we agree strongly on the need to gear the educational system as closely as possible to the pattern of job requirements. This can be helped by forecasting work, and even more by keeping a close eye on the current labour market. Why do more universities not study their graduates systematically to see whether the courses they teach are proving useful in employment? Models have their place in this, but the figures they generate need to be used with very great care.

1. See p. 66.

Charles Carter
Variety and Vision

The functions of institutions of higher education

The institutions of higher education do more than teach; and, in order to understand their nature, we need a better definition of their other functions. These are often lumped together as Research. In fact, it is often now believed that the universities (in particular) have always and necessarily been great centres of research, and that the time of the teacher should be spent in roughly equal parts on his teaching and his research. Historically this is nonsense; and indeed the whole matter is made almost meaningless by the careless application of the word 'research' to activities which are not all of the same nature. We ought to distinguish six different activities which take place in institutions of higher education, in addition to teaching:

1. Research, or the systematic search for new knowledge: typically the activity of the scientist in his laboratory, the historian working on a manuscript previously unstudied, the sociologist making surveys.

2. Development, or the making ready of previously discovered knowledge so that it may be of practical use.

3. Philosophical speculation, or the erection of new arguments on principles of logic, which is 'discovery' of what the mind can create.

4. Artistic creation, which in a broader sense is the discovery of what human beings can, out of their experience, add to the universe.

5. Scholarship, or the careful study of knowledge or of works of art or philosophical speculations already in existence. This may be a necessary condition of research, or speculation, or artistic creation; and the scholar who simply knows much and gives it out in his teaching is not to be despised.

6. Conservation, or the storage of accumulated human knowledge and experience, so that it may be re-examined in the

circumstances of a new generation. This is the work, essential to scholarship, of the librarians and bibliographers, who are the 'storekeepers' of science and culture.

All of these are activities which are undertaken with success outside the institutions of higher education: that is to say, it is not *necessary to their existence* that they should be linked to higher education, though that link may be convenient. But to what extent is it necessary to the effectiveness of higher education that these activities should take place within the same institution, and to some extent be undertaken by the teachers themselves? There is obviously some validity in the argument that a person who is a lively and effective teacher will want to be discovering things for himself. He will not be satisfied to hand out to students, year after year, a stock of ideas which is no longer growing or changing. We often confuse ourselves, however, by illegitimate extensions of the argument: for instance, that all teachers should want to be discovering *new* things (whereas some of the very best teachers are scholars who are not original creators); or that all teachers should want to be discovering new *knowledge*, that is, engaging in research, to the exclusion of philosophical speculation or artistic creation.

Let us therefore look a little further at the six activities and their relation to teaching in higher education. First of all, this teaching will certainly require convenient access to extensive library resources (a term which can be used broadly to include visual material, tape recordings, data banks, etc. as well as books). The need for a large library arises in part from the fact that, in the terminal years of full-time education, the interests of students 'fan out' into an enormous variety of specialist subjects. A more important point is that it is a valuable method of education at this stage that students should find things out for themselves, and not be tied to set textbooks or reading lists. By 'playing at scholarship' they learn what is certainly of use in later life, how to use the methods of scholarship to solve a problem. The library available to an institution of higher education must therefore be more than a collection of set texts; the needs of students will overlap those of scholars and researchers. Full research collections, of course, cannot possibly be available in every institution; there must be specialization, local and regional sharing and cooperation, a planned series of libraries of differing degrees of comprehensiveness. Nevertheless there exists, as a consequence of the needs of students, a close and necessary connexion between higher education and the activity of 'conservation' – an activity whose value is underestimated, for we often forget how much of the great achievements of humanity would be lost to memory without the protective care of libraries.

Once this connexion is established, it follows that 'scholarship' in the sense defined above becomes a natural activity of the institution. There will be individual scholars and groups of scholars centred on, say, the British Museum library, rather than the library of a teaching institution. But it is natural and convenient that scholarship should be well developed in the teaching institutions, and should enliven and improve their teaching. It is equally natural for research and philosophical speculation to be found there; though there is a tendency to overrate research relative to scholarship. This is perhaps the consequence of the false worship of 'originality': the discovery of a trivial fact previously unknown is given greater weight than a profound knowledge of important ideas. Original discovery earns Ph.D. degrees; mere scholarship is a reason for demoting a Ph.D. candidate to a Master's degree.

The other two activities are, in contrast to research, probably underrated by those concerned in higher education. Although many academics neither dwell in ivory towers, nor think them desirable places of residence, there is still in some places a class division between 'pure' research (the use of the emotive adjective is significant) and its application. In some cases at least, the best person to carry through the development of an idea is its originator, and it is desirable in the national interest that the institutional arrangements in higher education should be such as to encourage development.[1] Our failure to provide these arrangements is one reason for the belief (which is indeed exaggerated, but has some foundation) that 'Britain discovers and foreigners apply'.

1. The development companies of the Universities of Lancaster, Leeds and Loughborough provide an example. They exist not merely to hold patents on ideas created in the universities, but actively to pursue their development and use.

The reason for the relative neglect of artistic creation – which is an element of civilization so essential that surely educated men should be encouraged to appreciate it and to develop their own creative powers – is, I suspect, a particularly bad one: namely, that it does not provide a typical, examinable academic subject. Art and music are school subjects which all but a few gifted enthusiasts will give up before getting down to the serious grind of 'A' level work. At universities and colleges the creative arts are studied by a minority with a professional interest in them; in universities, even this professional study is sometimes historical and critical rather than creative. We produce considerable numbers of people able to talk critically about the great works of English literature, but pitiably few who have learnt the discipline of writing their own language well. In the fine arts, music and drama, what ought to be available to many as a part of general education is confined to a few.

The seven activities of teaching, research, development, philosophical speculation, artistic creation, scholarship and conservation thus all have a part to play in the institutions of higher education. But this tells us nothing about the proportions in which they should exist – in practical terms, the amounts of money which should be spent on them. There is no basis whatever for the assumption that 50 per cent of the time of a university teacher should be spent on 'research', but only (perhaps) 20 per cent of the time of a teacher in a polytechnic, and a negligible share of the time of a teacher in a college of education. It is certainly quite indefensible to suppose that 'research' should expand in strict proportion to teaching requirements, as though the meat of teaching and the wool of research were joint products of the academic sheep, present in inflexible proportions. On the other hand, sudden changes in the mix of activities are difficult to introduce, because expectations about this mix form part of the net attractiveness of particular jobs. For instance, it is sometimes suggested that the proportion of research activity in universities should be reduced by concentrating research in selected departments, and making the rest into teaching departments with a minimum of other scholarly activity. But, such is the prestige of research (particularly in science), and so great the attractiveness of being free to make one's name in research, that the result would be to attract the best minds to the institutions where they would have the least time to teach. A few, of no less ability but with a primary interest in teaching, would be attracted the other way, to the teaching-centred departments; but it would be unrealistic to suppose that the overall effect would be anything other than a selection to the disadvantage of teaching.

Some principles of organization

Having looked at the complexity of the possible functions of institutions of higher education, let us now consider some broad principles of organization. Of course, what can be done with higher education in the 1970s will be greatly influenced by what now exists. It will not be possible to demolish the University of Cambridge, or even to make more than minor deviations in its ancient practices. But, to get our minds clear, let us first consider some characteristics of the system we would create if we had the opportunity of a fresh start.

Higher education in Britain as it now exists is dominated by the first-degree course, taking three or four years of from twenty-four to thirty weeks of full-time formal study. The main variant is the sandwich course in its various forms, such as six-month periods of formal study interleaved with six-month periods of practical experience. On this as base are built Master's degree courses taking one or two years, and the lower doctorates (Ph.D. degrees) commonly taking three years. At this graduate level the 'period of study' becomes less clearly determined; for while undergraduates are known to do on average relatively little effective study in their extensive vacations, graduate students often work straight through the year. The three-year certificate courses for teachers are structured very much like first degrees, with somewhat shorter holidays: the diploma and other degree-equivalent courses in further education institutions are often similar in their structure to part-time or sandwich degree courses.

The average length of course in universities, in colleges of education and in advanced further education (full-time and sandwich courses) lies in each case between three and four years – after allowing for those who drop out and for those who take more than the minimum time. A first obvious question is why we should not have a considerable proportion of *two*-year courses. One year may be too short a time for adaptation to a new kind of study, after the years at school; but surely the population of possible entrants must include some who would benefit by two years of higher education, but for whom the extra benefit of a third year does not justify the cost or the use of time. (Unfortunately, three years of study are seen as a matter of prestige – as is well shown by the colleges of education, some of whose entrants have certainly gone as far as they will go after two years.) It is therefore worth considering whether we should not insert into the system some two-year 'junior colleges', giving a qualification different from the first degree, but with provision for the transfer of promising students to the degree and degree-equivalent courses.[1] These junior colleges would provide for a group whose apparent ability or degree of motivation lie at the margin at which it is doubtful whether they should commit themselves to a three-year course.

Another possibility is that the period of formal study should be extended beyond thirty weeks. The present vacations in universities are an adaptation of those at Oxford and Cambridge, which appear to be a survival from an age when the rich migrated from town to their country seats for the summer, and the poor were needed to help with the hay-making and the harvest. It is no excuse to say that university teachers get stale after eight or ten weeks of teaching; the timetable of an individual teacher can be adjusted to a length of course different from the length of a term. The question we ought to be examining is 'What is the optimum period of study in a year, from the point of view of educational value received?' – remembering that some at least of vacation activities (e.g. foreign travel) have their own educa-

1. This is different from the proposal, associated with the name of Professor A. B. Pippard, to open the universities to a large number of entrants taking a two-year degree, after which a selected number (perhaps a third) would continue with graduate studies. The difficulty about Professor Pippard's proposal is that a 'degree' (perhaps especially in his own University of Cambridge) has a meaning beyond the measurement of acquired knowledge : it signifies the completion of a maturing process in a civilized environment. Three years of Cambridge life cannot be packed into two; so that Professor Pippard's graduates would not be comparable to their predecessors, and should not receive the same title of Bachelor of Arts.

tional value. Since there is no known answer to this question, we ought to welcome experiments with different periods of study – say, thirty-five or forty weeks. However, this would not lead in any easy or simple manner to a reduction in the total length of a course. Without restructuring the whole of school education, it would be hard to get away from a once-a-year entry. But a three-year course cannot normally be compressed into two years: first, because forty-five weeks of formal study would almost certainly be too much; and second, because the process of education involves time, as well as quantity of instruction. It is difficult (except with some sandwich courses) to devise a course taking (say) two-and-a-half years, without wasting both teaching resources and capital equipment during the spare half-year before the next entry arrives. However, there is often pressure to *lengthen* existing courses to take account of increased knowledge or to provide extra 'breadth'; rather than go up from three to four years, each of thirty weeks, it would be well worth considering a change to a course, still of three years, but of forty weeks. (The planners often forget, in proposing four-year degrees, that a reduction of one year of working life is a significant economic burden – one year's less earning, and for many a prolongation of at least a partial dependence on their parents.) Perhaps, too, the discipline of longer terms and shorter holidays would be a better introduction to working life.

The relationship of higher education to working life deserves further consideration. At present we have a large number of courses which are in one sense an extension of school: that is to say, they are taken before a commitment to a particular career is made. We have other courses which intermingle academic study with work: and others again (the 'post-experience' courses) which are taken after a period of paid employment. It has long been thought that the demand for 'refreshment' or 'updating' would grow greatly in the coming years, in response to the greater speed of change of technology and of business methods. But this is only one example of the need for a greater fluidity of relationship between 'education' and 'work'. Apart from the planned sandwich courses, it would be useful to allow students to take courses by stages, with intervals of their own choosing for paid work; to mix full-time and part-time study; to go some way by part-time study in the Open University, and then transfer to full-time study; and so on. There would be many administrative difficulties, but it is very desirable to get away from the idea that 'education' is a once-for-all process of charging the batteries on which one will run for the rest of one's life.

We also need courses which stand in many different forms of relationship to the perceived requirements of particular vocations. Some will continue to be planned in direct relationship to a particular kind of work; for instance, the training of computer programmers, or some parts of teacher training. Some will have a more tenuous relation to work – an example is the training of a chemist, in relation to the needs of the chemical industry; but here there may be a need for 'bridging courses', to ease the transfer from a more general and academic study to work related to a specific industrial process. Some courses will have particularly in mind the possibility of changing the order of things which exists: an example is the study of social problems, which may well lead to the conclusion that partial remedies are not so important as an attack on fundamental causes. Many courses will continue to be non-vocational, concerned with a general training of the mind and enlargement of the understanding, the results of which can be used in many different ways. Obviously these forms of vocational relationship already exist; what is not always realized is the extent to which they coexist within the same institution, so that it is not possible to categorize some institutions as 'vocational' and others as 'non-vocational'.

It follows from what I have said that there is a complex interrelation of teaching with research, development, philosophical speculation, artistic creation, 'scholarship' and 'conservation'; and the effort given to these functions will (and should) vary, not only between institutions, but between people and departments in the same institution. One should not assume a set relation between the vocational emphasis of the teaching, and the nature of the non-teaching work of the institution. There is no necessary implication that 'non-vocational' means 'unpractical'; teachers of non-vocational courses can and do engage in research, development or other creative work of direct practical benefit to the community, and teachers of vocational courses engage in speculation far from immediate application. It is good that this should be so, for the interaction of long-run speculation and immediate practicality is of benefit to the intellectual life of an institution, and so to its teaching.

The nature of the education given

The central principle of organization, then, is that there should be abundant variety between and within institutions. What can be said about the nature of the education to be given? The answer must be relative, both to the qualities which higher education is intended to develop, and to the nature of the previous education of the entrants.

It sometimes seems that higher education is intended to develop the quality of being able to pass a final examination, and if one asks what the final examination is testing, it is impossible to obtain a clear answer. Obviously an examination can test whether, on a particular day, a student knows certain facts or can use certain methods, but few would think that this was the sum-total of the purposes of education. In a vaguer way, some kinds of examination or assessment test the ability to analyse a problem, originality in devising solutions, critical judgement, ability to see what is important, endurance or stamina, and other mental qualities. It is seldom clear, however, just what connexion is perceived between the qualities tested and those thought desirable in later life. A man may have first-class honours, but there is no answer to the question 'First-class for what?'

It is the nature of almost all forms of examination and assessment that structure tyrannizes over purpose. The assessment has to be capable of being made reasonably quickly, in a manner on which different assessors will not disagree too widely, and without the opportunity to cheat. Therefore a class of work is identified as 'examinable', and work which is not readily examinable will go untested, however important it may be. For instance, examiners commonly try, if they can, to avoid judgements about the quality of artistic creation. This would not matter so much if assessment were seen to be only a partial test, relating to that which is easily examinable; but unfortunately examinations reach back and distort the syllabus, or affect the motivation of the student so that he only works hard on those things which he knows will be examined.

Since high performance in an examination is treated as a qualification to teach in higher education (often regardless of any actual ability or training in the business of teaching), examinations provide a means of 'natural selection', rejecting those who are interested in the non-examinable, unless they have also mastered the examinable. Hence the professional boundaries of disciplines come to be drawn in odd places, excluding much that is of great relevance to a civilized life, and including much that is of less value. Economics, for instance, has long ceased to justify Marshall's description, 'a study of mankind in the ordinary business of life'; a great part of the profession spends its time in logical exercises of no relevance to the ordinary business of life, and, as a training of the mind, inferior to pure mathematics.

For the reason suggested in the last paragraph, but perhaps also by the accidents of history in the creation of professional sub-cultures, the academic community in Britain offers a partial and distorted education. It is partial, in that important subjects capable of serious study are left out, and distorted, in that the stress is laid in the wrong places. You do not succeed, as an economist, in obtaining the esteem of the profession by being interested in mankind in the ordinary business of life; it is far better to be the creator of an irrelevant and unusable (but ingenious and elegant) model of an economic growth process. Sir Walter Moberly's condemnation is still almost as valid as when he published it in *The Crisis in the University* in 1949:[1]

Our predicament then is this. Most students go through our universities without ever having been forced to exercise their minds on the issues which are really momentous. Under the guise of academic neutrality they are subtly conditioned to unthinking acquiescence in the social and political *status quo* and in a secularism on which they have never seriously reflected. Owing to the prevailing fragmentation of studies, they are not challenged to decide responsibly on a life-purpose or equipped to make such a decision wisely. They are not incited to disentangle and examine critically the assumptions and emotional attitudes underlying the particular studies they pursue, the profession for which they are preparing, the ethical judgements they are accustomed to make, and the political or religious convictions they hold. Fundamentally, they are uneducated.

1. SCM Press, 1949, p. 70.

The subtle conditioning to 'unthinking acquiescence' no longer works so well with the rebellious young; but it remains true that higher education too often evades the scholarly study of momentous issues, and leaves even those with a rebellious spirit in possession only of shallow and confused arguments and false notions.

In considering the nature of the higher education to be offered in the 1970s, therefore, it is well to start from a vision of the whole civilized man, and to let the practical constraints limit the educational choice only when one has formed a definite idea of what *ought* to be. The constraints will in fact be very limiting: they include not only the set ideas of professional groups of teachers whose membership can vary only slowly, but also the capacity of students to absorb ideas and to change attitudes during the limited period of a course. It is in this context that we have to assess the old controversy between 'depth' (or specialization) and 'breadth'. An apparently unanswerable case can be made for both. A broad education is especially needed because the structure of British school examinations tends to limit the active attention of sixth-form pupils to a narrow specialist range. It does not seem likely that this will alter much during the 1970s. It is needed, too, because the demands made in working life cannot be limited to the bounds of single academic subjects. Of course few men can be professional experts in several fields; but there is an intermediate state, in which enough links are created with other subjects to provide some imaginative understanding of the way in which they are developed, and to provide a means of enlarging that understanding when this is required. Whereas an educated man in Britain is hardly likely to be totally ignorant of English literature, it is still possible for him to be almost totally ignorant of scientific method, to react to statistics and mathematical models with alarmed incomprehension, and to know no more of the social sciences than the half-truths he picks up from his Sunday paper. It is also possible for him to be a Philistine in relation to the arts, or a bemused follower of fashion without any real critical feeling.

But (the supporters of specialization will reply) all this can only be corrected at the cost of an intolerable fragmentation of studies, so that the quality of mind achieved by going deep into a subject would no longer be present. The assumption that profound study on a narrow front does in fact produce a desirable quality of mind deserves to be questioned, but it must at least be conceded that the course made up of 'a little bit of everything' can easily be so superficial that the powers of the student are not tested or developed. For education in the methods and ways of thinking of a professional subject necessarily involves time and repeated exposure; it cannot be obtained easily.

Within a short period of study, the only thing to do is to compromise: to provide for some study in depth of a limited area, but also for some opportunity of breadth. But since the room for compromise is limited, it is necessary to be realistic about the priorities among the many alternative broadening agents. There should no doubt be great diversity of experiment and opportunity, but personally I hope that priority will be given to the systematic study of matters which are difficult and which bear on human survival, happiness and cultural advance. These include the impact of advanced technology on society; the relations of nation-states; the problems of human relationship, particularly in the family and in urban society; and the determination of aesthetic standards. The purpose of studying such matters is not to reach final conclusions, but to acquire the tools, basic ideas and mental processes necessary to continue their study throughout life. If the school system changes so as to provide such tools more effectively at the higher levels, there will be less to be done in higher education; but I cannot conceive that in the 1970s it will be right to plan initial higher education courses which are narrow in their specialization.

Some part of the function of encouraging the development of the whole civilized man is carried, not by any formal courses, but by the general life and environment of the institution: by student societies, by the traditional arguments over the midnight pint of beer, by chances to practise the arts and to see or hear beautiful things, by the opportunity to browse in a great library. Alternatively, of course, a different kind of development may be achieved by the discipline of a working environment for those engaged in sandwich and part-time courses: less broad in its opportunities, but with the advantage which comes from a greater responsibility. These extra-curricular influences must not be underestimated – as they often are, by those who suggest that all those who can pass the same examination are equally educated. If we had national degree examinations, taken by students at Oxford, Bradford, the polytechnics, the technical and commercial colleges offering degree courses, and the Open University, we surely would not think that the results represented, in all these institutions, exactly the same education. On the contrary, the Oxford student would still be sought after by some, in the belief that the traditions and influences of an ancient university had had an effect in making him a more civilized man; while others would esteem, for instance, the student who had 'come up the hard way' by part-time study in a technical college. Perhaps, however, we would get a better educational result if we encouraged a reasonable spread of extra-curricular influences, but also a discipline of hard work and an exposure to real-life decisions, in all institutions.

One important difference between institutions is in the proportion of their students who are living away from home. This is an important educational influence in itself, both because detachment from the home environment pushes students into new responsibilities – and maturity is gained in the act of facing these responsibilities – and because it is often easier to work and to make full use of extra-curricular facilities if one is away from home and from school friends. (The latter is particularly true of women students who tend, if at home, to be conscripted for domestic service.) But residence away from home is expensive: is it worth-while? It is impossible to give a clear answer to this question – how can one weigh non-measurable benefits against measurable costs? – but at least one can say that the present system does not select for residence away from home those who are most likely to need it, that is, those that come from a rather limited home background. It would not be difficult to amend the system of student grants so that the incentive to live at home became greater the higher the income of the parent – this would involve applying different means tests to grants for residence at home and away from home.

Peter Venables
Seven Principles for Expansion

Seven principles for expansion

We must examine what general principles and considerations should govern this expansion of tertiary education, not in the abstract, but from the complexities, defects and virtues of the system outlined in chapter 3. In doing so we have to keep in mind the considerable size of the growth foreshadowed in chapter 2. Seven major points need to be made, and though some will undergo revaluation in a changing political scene, they will nevertheless remain significant.

1. Whatever the changes that may come, we must assume that *greater economy and efficiency will be reasonably maintained* throughout the system. Thus there should surely be a more effective concern with the causes of students' success and failure, and with the transference of students to more suitable courses within the same or other institutions. Likewise there must be increased concern with the effectiveness of teaching, with induction and refresher courses for staff, and a greater use of modern technological aids to teaching. Tertiary institutions must adapt themselves to the necessities of life, indeed take a lead in these respects. These are not to be arrogantly dismissed as 'technological Benthamism'[1] because they challenge traditional assumptions and practices, for example, changing staff–student ratios in universities as a result of the advantages of new methods.

Considerations of cost effectiveness will be regularly applied to the establishment of courses and to the utilization of capacity of buildings, special equipment and facilities. Wasteful duplication between institutions must be avoided, and regional factors are likely to become much more important in this regard. National economic necessity will require these things to be done, but there is an awkward dilemma here for all parts of tertiary

1. F. R. Leavis, '*Literarism* versus *Scientism*: the misconception and menace', *The Times Literary Supplement*, 23 April 1970.

education, and not solely for the universities, as may be argued by some on elitist grounds. The avoidance of duplication may be economical and efficient, but care will have to be taken that this does not simply favour the development of a few centres of excellence at the expense of suppressing the emergence of excellent developments elsewhere. A strict, unimaginative application of the foregoing conditions will be apt to inhibit innovation, which could in the long run be disastrous.

2. No longer can any institution aspire to embrace the whole range of knowledge and skills; there is *a great diversity of institutions, and recent trends indicate that their functions in future will tend to overlap to a greater extent than in the past.* Such trends towards diminishing the distinctive differences between institutions were noted in the Report of the Select Committee on Education and Science (1968–9) on *Student Relations.* The report made a series of 'transbinary' comparisons between universities on the one hand, and 'the other sector of higher education within further education', which may be summarized as follows. Formerly, universities were distinct because they alone were empowered to grant degrees, but other institutions now grant awards which are degree-equivalent. Universities still enjoy an autonomy not shared by non-university institutions, but although in complete control over what they taught, their representatives impressed on the committee the importance of independent control by external examiners. The courses at non-university institutions were more specialized and vocational, but the creation of technological universities has made the distinction less rigid. Moreover, the range of courses in non-university colleges has widened, and many approximate closely in kind to conventional degree courses. Formerly non-university colleges recruited students largely or solely from the immediate locality, but many of the larger ones now draw students from further afield, regionally, and in some cases nationally. The distinctions are likely to become increasingly less significant as the polytechnics develop. While the local character of the non-university colleges is becoming less and less significant in distinguishing them from universities, universities are becoming more conscious of the importance of their association with local interests. In addition to noting these changes, the committee also felt that other

differences should be substantially reduced or removed. Examples they mentioned were the inequalities of provision of social and student union facilities, the inequalities in the provision for and conditions of service of staff, and the wide differences in attitudes towards student failure rates.

The doctrine of diminishing differences was taken a stage further by the Secretary of State, Edward Short, who replied to a question in the House of Commons about selection on 13 November 1969:

We have set up a number of polytechnics which are comprehensive institutions of higher education. I share the view of the Minister of Technology that eventually we shall have comprehensive universities as well.

This was amplified in April 1970:

The polytechnics are, of course, comprehensive institutions of higher education in both the composition of the student body and in the range and content of courses. A number of universities possess these characteristics to some extent. These are not matters of structural change imposed from outside, but of the natural growth and development of academic communities. I greatly welcome the growing tendency of universities to diversify in these and other ways.... What I hope is that over the years the universities will become increasingly comprehensive, both in the structure of the student body – part-time, full-time, sandwich courses and so on – and also in the level of their courses, having not only degree courses but also sub-degree courses.

It is well to be clear about the meaning of the much used word 'comprehensive', lest the debate becomes incomprehensible. Ordinarily it means 'characterized by comprehension; comprising or including much; of large content or scope; and characterized by mental comprehension'. The *Concise Oxford Dictionary of Current English* (1964) defines the comprehensive school as a 'large secondary school providing courses of varied kinds and lengths'. Latterly, however, it has acquired the meaning of 'all-inclusive', describing schools which include the *whole* age group in the catchment area. As the statements of the Secretary of State were made in response to questions about selection, which were in effect about moving selection from eleven- to eighteen-plus, the intention is clearly to apply the wider 'all-inclusive' meaning of 'comprehensive' to the polytechnics. This does not accord with the facts, for polytechnics do not include all the relevant age group, nor does the composition of the student body comprise, so far as it is known, the whole range of student ability in statistically significant terms. Neither are the polytechnics comprehensively all-inclusive in the range and content of their courses: to be so they must *all* provide undergraduate and postgraduate tuition in *all* the subjects in *all* the universities, which is manifestly inaccurate, not to say absurd. They have no medical faculties, nor have they law or arts or social science faculties on any scale comparable with the universities. The implication that the universities are less comprehensive in the range of their studies, which include postgraduate courses and research, and that they must in due time approach the ideal comprehensiveness of the polytechnics, is all of a piece with the implication of the binary policy that the universities are not responsive to social needs. The same is true of the assertion about sub-degree work, for this is certainly not all contained in the polytechnics. This level of work was not defined, but on any definition, it should at least include a great deal of the work of area colleges, and perhaps also of local colleges of further education. A few, less than half a dozen, departments of education have been established in the regional colleges/polytechnics in the last two or three years, and this is hardly a justifiable basis for a claim to comprehensiveness, in comparison with the work of long-established departments of education in the universities, and their substantial responsibilities for teacher-training colleges, later colleges of education, following the McNair Report of 1946.

If 'comprehensive' has the more restricted scope already noted, then why all the competitive pother? Is the definition 'comprising much; of large content or scope; providing courses of varied kinds and lengths' not an accurate description (so far as it goes) of polytechnics *and* universities (but not of colleges of education)? Defined thus more modestly, the consequential questions relate to *comprising how much*: that is, to what kind of content and scope each institution should have, within what is (as a plain matter of fact) a great diversity of provision. There is an ambivalence about diversity and unity in tertiary education as uneasy as that about equality and excellence. 'Can we be equal and excellent too?' was the question posed by John L. Gardiner's book,[1] and we may add, 'Can we be diversified and unified too? Can we be diverse and unitary too?' While differences between institutions will diminish in certain respects, each as a progressive enterprise will retain its particular orientation and individual characteristics. These will come mainly out 'of the natural growth and development of academic communities', but also in response to external needs and influences, and some at least will be reinforced by the attempt to achieve a national allocation of scarce resources to the best advantage. If conditions are such that a rich diversity of institutions is fostered within tertiary education as a whole, then competitive claims that this or that sector or this or that institution is more comprehensive than any other become meaningless. The important thing is to secure the interrelatedness of diverse institutions, and already we are passing from a phase of *in*dependent autonomous institutions to *inter*-dependent institutions – witness the sharing by universities of nuclear facilities and computing services, and their joint establishment of a variety of postgraduate courses.

3. In the major expansion of university education in the United Kingdom during the last decade, ten universities were formed by the granting of charters to existing institutions, two resulted by a splitting of existing universities, and nine began as entirely new ventures. The question is what balance of new and evolved institutions will best meet the needs of the future. Perhaps we need an Occam's Razor for the next expansion : 'Let the number of educational institutions be not unduly multiplied.' Full regard should be had to the critical mass effect, below which neither institutions nor departments can function effectively at reasonable cost. The proliferation of small institutions should be avoided and, for other reasons given in point 5 (p. 95), the size of many institutions should be substantially increased. Existing universities ought to be increased to the maximum capacity of their sites, and those that can readily expand still further on

1. *Can We Be Equal and Excellent Too?*, Harper & Row, 1961; paperback 1962.

adjacent sites should be enabled to do so. As far as is necessary the same should apply to the polytechnics. Very large institutions have their dangers and defects; they have become evident enough, and we need to guard against them. But institutions which are too small have their inadequacies also and these, being long-term in effect, are likely to remain hidden. In the expansion a prime consideration should be to establish an effective minimum size of departments, and where this is not possible, small units should be transferred elsewhere. While proper consideration would have to be given to the human aspects of particular changes, an ineffective and disproportionately expensive diversity must be avoided. The greatest gain in staff–student ratios would probably result from expansion on these lines.

4. 'Let diversity within institutions increase effectively within the means available.' Not an impossible, unmanageable diversity within *all* institutions, but a diversity arising from planned additions and reorientations on a sufficient scale. As to the specialist and generalist functions of institutions, increasing pressures should not be allowed to separate them, but a changing balance between them must be achieved. Thus the universities should not, as some urge defensively by oversimplification, re-treat into an elitist research function and jettison their existing generalist functions elsewhere. On the contrary, the generalist function is becoming increasingly important, partly because many students understandably do not wish to make a definite vocational commitment at the outset of their career, in a highly complex and perplexing world. Moreover, the impact of science and technology and of mass media and communications is paradoxically placing an increasingly greater value on generalist education. There is a need to add a generalist function to many existing specialist institutions.

5. A single or narrow vocational purpose is no longer a suffi-cient justification for an institution of higher education, and *multi-purpose institutions are an inescapable necessity* for the following main reasons:

(a) The changing nature of society and employment, and the increasing difficulty of prediction of changes.

(b) The increasing requirements for literacy and numeracy and of interdisciplinary understanding, with which go deferred specialization, wider groupings of cognate studies, and an increasing proportion of common and combined courses.

(c) The increasing necessity of re-education of mature employees from time to time, to keep them up to date. This recurrent re-investment in their higher education can be either in specific disciplines, as in the physical sciences, or it can be for different groups pursuing related studies together, as in the social sciences for those engaged in personal service occupations.

(d) A certain minimum provision of cognate studies, with adequate staff and facilities, is essential for interdisciplinaary courses to be effective.

There are encouraging trends towards multi-purpose institutions already apparent. Recently the Association of Technical Institutions, established in 1893, resolved to re-name itself as the Association of Colleges of Further and Higher Education. The colleges of education also wish to widen their functions,[1] but these are, however, closely related to the emergence of a graduate teaching profession (see p. 135). They have even been articles suggesting that the educational functions of the polytechnics are not wide enough for future needs,[2] and that the name may prove inadequate and misleading.

6. On educational and political grounds, there is a *necessity to ensure an adequate number of safety valves* in the educational system. Despite the highest standards of selection and examination, the processes are inevitably subject to varying degrees of error. Moreover, people mature at different rates and in the educational process maturation and motivation are of profound importance. In addition, adverse social conditions will continue to reduce educational opportunities for many in each age-group, and the system of tertiary education should therefore afford many different routes for the flow of ability – full-time, sandwich, block-release and part-time courses – and of effective links between them. The system should become less part-time in character, and the provision of full-time and sandwich courses needs

1. *Higher Education and Preparation for Teaching: A Policy for Colleges of Education*, Association of Teachers in Colleges and Departments of Education Report, 1970.

2. See D. W. Jary, 'General and vocational courses in polytechnics, with special reference to sociology', *Universities Quarterly*, Winter 1969.

to be substantially increased, as well as block-release courses of longer duration than at present.

7. We must *encourage and record excellence*, firstly by intelligent imaginative planning; but there are other ways of ensuring that the particular excellence and purpose of each institution is preserved in a richly diverse system of tertiary education. At present, very desirable conditions of governance and academic responsibility, of conditions of service and amenities, are enjoyed by a very small group of institutions and are substantially denied to the rest; even the hope of attaining them on prescribed standards of achievement is largely frustrated. So it becomes inevitable that the most worthwhile and ably staffed of the deprived institutions will persistently endeavour to modify, re-orientate, even distort their functions in the direction of the favoured few. If diversity of institutions is to be secured, indeed fostered, then institutions of proven worth should be clearly recognized as such by the system.

We have a variety of devices for approving or accrediting courses, but few for accrediting an institution as a worthy educational entity. However, recognition of sufficient courses by the Council for National Academic Awards does imply a kind of recognition of the institution as a whole, so why not have an explicit accreditation by the CNAA or other body of the requisite standing? With further proven attainments in the institution's own line of development, there should then follow the granting of a charter, not as a university, but as a chartered polytechnic, institute, college, or as some suitably federated institution. Each step would be accompanied by significant gains in academic responsibility, governance, finance and administration, i.e. in the degree of autonomy which is granted. At various stages of their development, the representatives of the colleges of advanced technology were emphatically assured that only chartered universities could grant degrees in the United Kingdom, but within a few years, following the Robbins Report, the power to grant degrees under a charter was granted to a non-university body, the CNAA. More recently, charters with such powers have been granted to the Royal College of Art and the Cranfield Institute of Technology, neither of which is a university. We may speculate as to what the position in higher education would have been at this present time had the colleges of Advanced Technology been treated similarly from 1956 onwards, and become chartered royal colleges of technology or royal polytechnics; and also whether the present policy concerning polytechnics would ever have been formulated. Be that as it may, there is little doubt that the two stages of accreditation, described above, would in future ensure a greater self-respect for institutions and mutual respect between them, not excluding universities, and would be an effective means of securing their most desirable diversity.

Points 4, 5, 6 and 7 are closely related aspects of a comprehensive *system*, and are of prime importance to maintaining the range of choices open to students. In a recent study by Stephen H. Spurr, the American B.A. degree is stated to represent

a broad degree gate, offering a wide range of non-invidious choice to a wide range of students ... [it] permits a progressive choice of career opportunities, and provides re-entry possibilities for those who wish to change their field as their interests, talents and motivations develop.

The argument is strongly in favour of flexibility, in line with the judgement that:

Too much effort has been expended upon the definition and establishment of mutually exclusive classes of institutions and discrete non-overlapping programs within these institutions.[1]

This applies in varying measure to parts of the British system, and to the dichotomy of the binary system, whereas a more open-ended flexible system, providing a more effective escalation of ability within and between institutions and courses, is required for future needs.

All the foregoing considerations demand an awareness of the hazards of recent proposals for reducing the costs of expansion.[2] One such proposal is that increased numbers should be

1. *Academic Degree Structures: Innovative Approaches: Principles of Reform in Degree Structures in the United States* (A General Report prepared for the Carnegie Commission on Higher Education), McGraw-Hill, 1970, pp. 22, 26.

2. See Committee of Vice-Chancellors and Principals, *University Development in the 1970s*, November 1969, reprinted in *Higher Education Review*, Spring 1970.

taken in part-time courses, despite the much higher failure rate that they entail. Another is that educational choice should be limited largely to local institutions, which would reduce mobility and deny the social benefits of residence away from home to the relatively underprivileged. The proposal that a year should be inserted between school and university would have the strong likelihood that only the more mature, the more intellectually/ socially/materially well-endowed will subsequently arrive at the doors (especially if it is merely an in-filling, off-putting year with no real educational purpose). Another recurrent proposal is that students' grants be replaced in whole or in part by students' loans, which would reduce still further the already low proportion in tertiary education at degree level of women students and of students from working-class homes. There is also the proposal that the number/proportion of postgraduate students – whether for Master's degrees or Ph.D. – should be reduced to some preconceived necessary level – a remarkable proposal indeed, when the need to defer specialization is important, and when whole sectors of industry and commerce are deficient in or even devoid of research insights or techniques.

Chapter Five
The Place of the Universities

Future policy for higher education is often seen as a conflict between universities and polytechnics. Earlier chapters will have suggested already that this must be a misleading over-simplification; nevertheless the differences in attitude between the leading institutions in the two parts of the binary system will no doubt be important. Here, then, are two sharply opposed views. George Brosan, director of a polytechnic, sees the existence of polytechnics as due to a remarkable social failure of universities: he quotes those who think that the interests of universities and of industry are divergent and at root irreconcilable. Charles Carter, vice-chancellor of a new university, considers that within the variety of the university system can be found the growing points for many new types of course and new methods of keeping close to practical reality. He sees advantage in the 'universality' and autonomy of universities. However, it is false to suppose that government has disturbed a tidy structure of degree studies in universities by creating polytechnics. The binary system was not created by act of policy; it evolved, as a consequence of allowing external degrees to be taken in further-education colleges. The creation of polytechnics can be seen as a necessary rationalization of what already exists. Therefore, although Brosan and Carter are clearly a long way from convincing each other (or even agreeing on the facts), the practical consequences of the disagreement may not be as far-reaching as they seem.

George Brosan
A Self-Limited Function

Polytechnics are new and their function is not defined. Universities for the most part are much older, yet their function is not defined either. Because of their greater maturity, universities have accumulated elegant prototypes of favoured activity which need to be examined to understand what polytechnics are about. This is the object of the present chapter.

The first and simplest thing to be said is that polytechnics owe their existence to universities in more senses than one. Most polytechnics at some prior stage in their development have been under the academic tutelage, or patronage, of a university, and in this sense the academic development of polytechnics owes much to the remarkable vigour of university intellect. That polytechnics exist at all is, however, the result of a correspondingly remarkable social failure of universities. The logistic development of polytechnics owes all to the failure of university involvement with society.

A necessary starting-point for justifying this statement is an examination of the objectives of each type of institution. One by now conventional starting-point for this sort of analysis is the Robbins Report; this deals by omission mainly with the work of universities and proto-universities. The Robbins Report early on considered the aims and objectives of higher education – what purposes and general social ends were proper to higher education. The report acknowledged a plurality of aims, and asserted that there were four objectives essential in a coherent higher education system. They were:

1. Provision of instruction in skills required for participation in the general division of labour. The attitude of the Report was that the utility of acquiring skills had to be recognized at least from the point of view of the student who was concerned in part with the value of his education 'in the maintenance of a competitive position'.

2. Promotion of the general powers of the mind – in the sense

of production of cultivated men and women, not mere specialists. This should be accomplished in conjunction with practical skills only if the latter are taught at a level and at a plane of generality which makes them suitable for wide application.

3. The advancement of learning, not in the sense of the balance between teaching and research, but rather in the sense of the search after truth being the essential function of a university and the commitment to education being valid when it is concerned with discovery.

4. Transmission of culture, that is, common standards of citizenship. Again this is not to be interpreted in the sense of imposing an unthinking conformity, but rather in the sense of providing a background of culture and social habit upon which a healthy society depends.

There is implicit in this last objective, and indeed in the previous ones, the assumption that no matter what was to be done by any present or future university, the essential need for maintenance of standards remained. Similar remarks are made in a broad way by the University Grants Council on the aims of university work.

First and foremost [among the qualities of mind which distinguish the educated person, it would place] . . . . a capacity to think, by which we mean not only the power of ratiocination but also and more particularly the ability to see the significance of facts and developments and their implications beyond the context in which they are first apprehended, and to exercise an independent judgement on the importance of facts and the quality of actions. The danger is that the utilitarian purpose of the special subject will drive the student to memorize as much as possible of this knowledge in the limited time available leaving him with no time to develop his power of thought or to acquire any knowledge outside this subject (*University Development 1952–1957*, 1958).[1]

It should not be thought, however, that the Robbins statement of aims is – for all its simplicity and commonsense appeal –

---

1. Nor should it be thought that these views are those of yesterday. Lord Todd, Chancellor of Strathclyde University, said in his Presidential address to the British Association in September 1970 that he did not believe that a traditional type of university education was appropriate for a large proportion of each age group; what the majority ought to pursue was some other form of higher education with a different and greater vocational bias.

one which is universally acceptable within the university system. A point of view expresed by, among others, Professor John Anderson is that it is logically wrong to assume it is possible to state the purposes of a university; a university simply does not belong to that class of social institutions which can be regarded as having a definable purpose. In a famous letter to *The Times* Professor Basil Mitchell says, in reply to the question of what universities are for:

Most university teachers in this country would, I think, give an answer something like this. A university is essentially a community of scholars (in a broad sense of the word) concerned with the disinterested pursuit of truth. As such it is bound to teach apprentice scholars their job, and it has also been entrusted with the task of educating students who are not going to be professional scholars. They are given the same sort of intellectual training as those who are, for a number of reasons; it's a tough intellectual training which sets an exacting standard; it represents an ideal of disinterested inquiry which is valued by a civilized society (and helps to make it civilized); it transmits to the student some part of our inherited culture and equips him to some extent to criticize it and contribute to it; it may also prepare him for a specific vocation.

This educational task is assisted by all the other activities which go on in a university, religious, political, artistic, athletic.

If something like this is what a university is for, it must, like the Church and the Arts, have more than a purely instrumental role. It cannot be regarded simply as a means of achieving social and economic aims, however important these are, or simply as a component part in the national system of education. Nor can it be expected to 'produce' people of some desired type, if this conflicts with the primary aim of enabling students to become genuinely 'self-moving'. And a university must be selective, since not everyone has the sort of talent or the degree of interest to sustain a university course. None of this automatically settles the practical issues that are being currently discussed, but it does create a strong presumption in favour of allowing universities (individually as well as collectively) the greatest possible independence. In so far as privileges are rights which an institution needs to have in order effectively to discharge its obligations to society, there is an important sense in which universities ought to be 'citadels of privilege'.

Support for the idea that the interests of universities and industry are at least divergent and, at root, irreconcilable, does not come only from classicists. Professor G. H. Rawcliffe, a distinguished electrical engineer who spent many years in industry before taking up university life, had this to say in his 1970 Hunter Memorial Lecture, given to the Institution of Electrical Engineers in London:

We in Bristol are firm supporters by practice as well as by precept of collaboration between universities and industry; but as the industrial and economic scene unfolds I am less and less convinced that this collaboration should take the form of persuading the best university men to move full time into industry. As time proceeds, industry seems to me to be more and more concerned with the problems of manufacture and organization. It is more and more market-oriented. I am perfectly prepared – with whatever reservations – to believe that this shift of industrial emphasis and activity is inevitable and very desirable; but it would be much better if the facts were generally recognized.

A good deal of misunderstanding has occurred in the past by the tacit assumption that the interests of universities and industry were identical. Neither can do without the other, that is quite certain, but their objectives and attitudes do not always coincide.

In some sense, the ideals of a university and industry are as the poles asunder. The touchstone of a university is knowledge – that of industry is action. Thought and action cannot be divorced, but the ideal of industry is the least thought with the most effect. . . . A university is apt to breed too great a regard for principle to be convenient for industrial life. . . .

I have quoted at length because it is apparent that, whatever differences there may be between, say, a classicist and an electrical engineer, there is a concensus between these two individuals on the need for some remoteness and some non-involvement with industry. The definition of the role of a university in terms of the generation and distribution of knowledge refers to views expressed in the last decade, not the last century. There are many examples; take the essay by Professor A. Phillips Griffiths, published as part of a collective work in 1965 on the philosophy of education.[1] It is erudite, enlivening and entertaining. In a carefully set-out argument Griffiths tries to show what a university essentially is, and how its essential nature pertains to other

1. R. Archambault (ed.), *Philosophical Analysis and Education*, Routledge & Kegan Paul, 1965.

functions it performs. These other functions are amusingly called 'accidents'. The essence of the university is the pursuit of learning, shown to be an end in itself and a justifiable one to boot; it is the Ideal. In order to pursue this Ideal the university has to *perpetrate* accidents (since presumably no one causes accidents on purpose), which include activities such as teaching, education, the pursuit of the useful arts, and preparation for life.

Teaching is an accident in a university because (according to Griffiths) valid teaching can only emerge from love of the subject, from concern for pupils as future academics rather than future 'wage-earners'; teaching is only relevant in the context of internal, not external, criteria; in any event no one can be instructed how to pursue truth other than by example ('sitting by Nellie' is perhaps a more apt phrase). Education is an accident because anyone who is not universally cultured is a barbarian. Useful arts are irrelevant because what matters is how learning is pursued, not the use to which it is put. Even the Platonic view that there are studies which ultimately produce good leaders is rejected; it is not the function of learning to cause changes in people.

Neither can it be assumed that these views apply only to the older and well-established universities. The new universities, despite their recent arrival on the scene, are basically similar to the older ones in respect of their philosophy. No one could mistake an embryo university in all its unready muddy-huttedness, however transient, for a technical college with identical lack of physical amenity. The new universities as well as the old are devoted to the traditional purposes of a university – the generation and transmission of knowledge. This is apparent in their organization, their style of academic leadership, their easy equating of 'good' with 'traditional'. Murray G. Ross, the editor and part-author of *New Universities in the Modern World*,[1] says:

The tradition of the university is to seek scholars for its faculty; to press for scholarly study, research and publication; and to insist on teaching by informed and speculative minds.... It is quite apparent from the preceding chapters that the new universities are firmly moored in this tradition....

There is much that is new and highly commendable in the

1. Macmillan, 1966.

new universities. They have not been slow to experiment with combinations of subjects, with methods of teaching, with delaying of specialization, and with the framework and organization of student life. But in the essential respect of philosophy they have remained invariant under the transformations of the society around them. They are concerned – properly from their viewpoint – with the generation and distribution of knowledge.

This theme is repeated elsewhere in Ross's book, and is made quite explicit. The University of East Anglia makes 'the traditional assumption that the object of the university is the pursuit of learning'. The University of Sussex justifies the need for academic autonomy on the grounds that 'the progress in freedom of society as a whole depends on the unfettered quest for truth within its universities'. The University of York concedes that it has a duty to 'train professionals', but is unclear as to which professionals should be trained in universities and which are 'more appropriately educated elsewhere'. The undifferentiated use of 'education' and 'training' is perhaps not as important as the assertion that the university obviously has a duty to transmit a tradition of culture and, more important, the obligation to discover, to teach and to re-interpret.

The universities have, of course, been under substantial attack for an alleged non-fulfilment of their function. This is not a new situation. One attack comes from the industrialists who, following Paul Chambers, say that the graduates are deliberately unfitted for industry. The other attack comes from university students, who assert that the normal, if unstated, goals of education in, say, literature – the assimilation of culture and tradition through the study and critical analysis of outstanding works – are too academically introspective. The cry for relevance is a result of the realization that such studies have failed to cause earlier generations to apply their knowledge and wisdom to the solution of urgent moral, philosophical and political problems. It is this lack of applied education in the non-technologies which is the crucial issue facing humanity; the failure is one of arts and humanities, not of technology.

The current strident demand by students for community-related studies is said by them to be a result of the lack of relevance of hitherto existing education. In the eyes of many students the universities have failed even to consider, let alone to meet, the challenge.

Universities have not taken up, or in some cases have withdrawn from, large areas of activity. There is considerable evidence – for example in the daily papers – that throughout the world, universities are increasingly leaving other types of institution much leeway to deal with teaching and learning that does not fit into the declared university pattern. For example, there are a variety of private organizations dealing with academically non-respectable functions such as salesmanship, marketing, computing, language learning and so on. In other areas the role is played differently; the growth of pure and applied research in many types of industrial organization, some specially set up for the purpose, is due to the different emphases of the industrially oriented pursuit of knowledge and the academically oriented pursuit of knowledge. In the UK the academic non-respectability of management education until recently is a case in point. From the point of view of society this diversification is probably not inherently bad.

It has been said, probably with some justification, that the trouble with people who philosophize about universities is that they are unduly influenced by what they read about universities, and do not pay enough attention to what actually goes on within the universities themselves. The argument here is that, in practice, the universities act in one way and are described as being motivated to act – by philosophers and others from within the universities – in quite another way.

If we decline to believe, as I do, that the scribes either are hopelessly myopic or are deliberate liars, we are forced to the conclusion that action in the universities in practice is not in accordance with any stated view on the purposes of a university. This psychological distance, if it exists, between declared concepts and observed action is at least logically odd. It is easier to assume that with a community of people of the highest intelligence, divergence in action will be inevitable, but that the overall purposes of a university, insofar as they have been stated, have been stated accurately. The key question is: if they have been *inaccurately* stated, why have they not been more effectively challenged?

Charles Carter
The Advantages of
Freedom and Diversity

It suits the enemies of the universities to represent them as
though they were all cast in the same mould, to resemble a
caricature of prewar Oxford and Cambridge – expensive, archaic
homes of privilege, resistant to change, selecting students on a
class basis, with courses little related to national needs. In fact,
however, it is the glory and strength of the British university
system that it is exceedingly diverse, and that in consequence it
is highly adaptable to new circumstances. If, for instance, it is
argued that there ought to be more applied courses closely related to the needs of particular industries – Leeds has been providing such courses for years, and so have many other places.
If it is argued that teaching and research should be problem-
centred, instead of being intellectual exercises undertaken for
their own sake – it is only necessary to look at some of the newer
engineering courses, or at the curricula and research of the
university business schools, to find excellent examples of the
problem-centred approach. If one seeks a curriculum concerned
with the unity of diverse disciplines, rather than with their
separate development – what else are Sussex, Keele and Lancaster doing? If one wants opportunities for mature students,
for part-time students, for students not prepared by ordinary
school examinations, they can all be found in the university
system – though it must be admitted that the provision for part-
time students is nowhere near great enough. So far from being
unresponsive to demands and resistant to change, the British
universities have shown themselves to be rather too anxious to
jump aboard the passing bandwagon. The shrewd university
man is looking all the time for the developments which will be
fashionable tomorrow, in the hope of getting in first and claiming the status of a pioneer, and this has led to a rush after
novelty (to be found in, for instance, subjects such as marketing,
materials science, environmental studies) which has not always
been well-advised. The critics often generalize falsely, from the

example of one university which has resisted one particular change, and fail to notice the several others which have accepted it.

As for being expensive, the universities have shown a willingness to understand the economics of their operations and to seek economies which should serve as an example to all State-financed enterprises. Their staff–student ratio is, when like is compared with like, no better than that in the rest of higher education; their junior staff are paid less (see p. 27). The apparently high cost per student is entirely accounted for by the attribution to students of the costs of research. University capital programmes similarly include a large contribution to the accommodation of research and development. As for extravagance, where in the public sector have people designed buildings at costs from 10 to 40 per cent below the government's cost norms? If the purpose of the teaching side of the universities is to produce students who are successful in obtaining degrees, where in the public sector (except in colleges of education) and where in other countries will one find dropout rates so low and final success rates so high? The true teaching cost of British universities per graduate produced is *not* high; it is strikingly low, for the nature of the education given.

It is easy to prove of universities, as of sixth forms, or of grammar schools, that the professional classes are over-represented among their students. The educational advantage of a middle-class home shows right from the beginning of the school years, with a cumulative effect which has become large by the age of eighteen. It would be quite impossible for universities, by a deliberate bias in favour of the lower socio-economic groups, to correct so massive an effect. Nevertheless, almost every university selector I have known has had *some* bias in favour of students whose limited social background suggests that they may have been handicapped in the rat-race of school examinations. This bias could be more effectively exercised if a university place were not a scarce commodity; but the selector is bound to consider not only the advantage of letting a student in, but also the injustice he is doing to another student who must in consequence be kept out.

In planning for an expansion of higher education the universities have some important advantages. One is simply their closer approximation to universality than is found in other institutions of higher education. The universities generally include or intend to include both vocational and non-vocational courses, and a broad sweep of subjects covering technology and applied and pure science, mathematics, historical and philosophical subjects, language and area studies, and the social sciences. They unite undergraduate and graduate work, teaching and research and 'conservation': students have considerable opportunity, not only to interact with and learn from those in other disciplines, but also to change their courses. Some elements of this universality are of course to be found in the polytechnics and elsewhere, but an opposite example is to be seen in the colleges of education: institutions tied to a single vocation, with limited opportunities of interaction and little chance for a student to change to another course (see p. 137).

Another great advantage of the universities is their autonomy. It has been interesting to watch the protagonists of the so-called Independent University (to be dependent on fees and private funds) putting forward the justification that the State-supported universities have lost or will lose their freedom. But there is little sign that any freedom has been or will be 'lost' except one which never really existed, namely the freedom to spend public money in unlimited quantities without accounting for the expenditure. And the Independent University will surely have at least the same accountability to the donors of its funds.

The universities are independent corporations established by royal charter, with wide powers of action. Their financial freedom is maintained at as high a level as is conceivable under any system of support, by the use of block grants decided for five-year periods, by the right to carry forward surpluses, and by the interposition between government and the individual university of a University Grants Committee, now highly professional but remaining receptive and sympathetic to university views. The freedom of universities includes the right *not* to follow government policy, and to establish or keep alive studies which may be highly unwelcome to the government. Since governments are not always right, it is desirable in the interests of all citizens that this freedom of inquiry and teaching should be protected. The universities provide, in fact, multiple points of decision on academic matters, where otherwise there might be only one point; for instance, the decision of a research council not to support a project or course may sometimes be grievously wrong, and it is desirable that someone should be able to snap his fingers at a central decision which he thinks misconceived. It is sometimes supposed that the control of universities is effected privily by the University Grants Committee. This is far from the truth: in normal circumstances only gentle expressions of opinion (usually wise and helpful) come from that body. In founding a new university at Lancaster, and bringing it to 2,900 students in its seventh year, I am not conscious of any occasion on which academic decisions, reasonably available to us within our budget, have been dictated from outside. Generally, one asks no one's permission before taking the important decisions about curriculum, the development of departments, the recruitment of staff, the admission of students and their assessment. Exceptionally, one is conscious of doing something with which the UGC might not wholly agree: but, if it is thought right, it is done – and presented with appropriate tact and finesse.

So complete a freedom attracts the adverse comment of another group of critics. This (they say) is wasteful anarchy: the universities as servants of the public ought to be under public control (whatever that means – the precise instrument of control is seldom stated). It must be admitted that freedom has been abused – an example is the injustice of the differing regulations for the Bachelor of Education degree in different parts of the country. But all real freedom must be *capable* of being abused; and the universities have done a great deal, in recent times, to introduce a sensible coordination of their activities, and to relate them to public policy, in so far as it is known. It is very unlikely that the B.Ed. muddle would be repeated if the decision had to be made today. There is still (as mentioned above) a tendency to adopt novelties in too many places too quickly, but this too is being restrained: for instance, a group of northern universities now exchange their quinquennial development plans at a formative stage, so as to discourage unwise competition. It is a matter of judgement whether the system operates at the right point, between the untidiness of freedom (which may nevertheless give the best chance for new ideas to grow) and the orderliness of a planned system (which may be economical, but can also be dull and unprogressive). Personally I think that the British universities have reason to be proud of their recent record of innovation, of research into their own activities, and of regard for economy and the public good; this suggests to me that we have got the balance between freedom and order about right.

If higher education were still (as it was in 1939) predominantly in the universities, then I believe that the needs of the 1970s could be met in a full and appropriate manner within the university system. There would have to be much adaptation – to new lengths and levels of course, to a different relation of teaching to research and to the other activities discussed on page 77; but I see no evidence that the university system would prevent this adaptation, or fail to carry it through with appropriate vigour. All the reasons now given for the development of a separate system of higher education in the polytechnics and colleges of further education appear to me to be excuses with no real validity – with a single exception. The single valid excuse is that the further-education sector has the desirable quality of being 'comprehensive', in one of the senses mentioned on page 92, namely by bringing together higher-education courses and more elementary courses such as those for the Ordinary National Certificate. As I shall suggest later, the question of 'comprehensiveness' is indeed central to future planning.

However, as university staff so often forget, the government has never had to face the issue of whether to create a binary system: it had one already, by a series of historical accidents, including the availability of London external degrees to students in colleges, and the establishment of degree-level professional courses growing out of the lower-level work of technical colleges. Viewed from the government side, the establishment of the polytechnics was a rationalization of a situation in which higher-level courses were scattered over a great number of colleges, with consequent low numbers and high costs.

The real issue, then, is how to accommodate ourselves to what exists: by separate development (and, in that case, where should the main development occur?), or by the integration of the two sectors. In chapter 7 I shall argue in favour of the latter course.

Chapter Six
Two Views of the Binary System

In the previous chapter George Brosan explained what
universities look like from his point of view. In doing this, he
develops a philosophical structure to explain the nature and need
for an array of institutions, and on this basis he would justify
the existence of separate planning of different sorts of institution,
such as the binary system provides. Peter Venables looks at the
various types of institution, and sees, not a tidy array, but a
substantial overlap of functions. He discusses the need for
teaching to become a graduate profession, and the desirability of
developing colleges of education into multi-purpose institutions.
He examines in some detail the latest information about the
plans and purposes of the Open University. He concludes (in
opposition to Brosan) that, while the binary system's origins are
understandable, it encourages anomalies and fosters vestigial
remains which no longer serve a useful purpose. It must be made
clear that none of the authors is arguing that the expansion of
the 1970s could or should take place in a single kind of
institution : all are in favour of variety, and indeed of more
variety than exists at present. The 'binary issue' is not about the
choice between uniformity and variety, but about the best method
of administering a diverse structure of institutions.

George Brosan
An Array of Institutions

Due to the differing roles of the universities and polytechnics, there is often talk of a spectrum of institutions, a hierarchy of esteem. The word 'spectrum' is a possible culprit in inducing a rather simple model of institutional ranking. In its professional sense spectrum means a series of images obtained when energy of some kind is resolved into its component parts. In its every-day usage it means a range of activities or ideas; but it is essentially a linear range. According to this, activities or ideas can be disposed on a straight line and thus placed in a unique rank-ing order or hierarchy. But there is no prior reason why we need limit our placement of ideas and functions to a single dimen-sion. A more useful model, it transpires, is two-dimensional. We can call it an array.

One obvious way in which institutions differ is in the degree of complexity and difficulty of the professional, techno-logical and theoretical work involved. For example, the work of the first-year student in electrical installation can loosely be described as being concerned with electrical engineering; so can the work of a research team in the Electrical Research Association exploring the interruption of currents in a vacuum; and so can the work of Ole Franksen in his search for a universal engineering language. These differ from each other in the relative difficulty of the concepts they involve and the degree of prior knowledge that is assumed in coping with the complexity. They differ, that is, in intellectual demands.

Not all courses in a single institution will make the same intellectual demands; even within a single department or pro-fessional school there will be differences. But insofar as the concept of differences in intellectual complexity is valid, it is possible pragmatically to rank them in some kind of order.

Another of the many ways in which institutions differ is in the social attitudes implicit in their work. A good deal has already been said about this for both universities and polytechnics. Various courses may be concerned to a greater or lesser extent with the application of knowledge; in theory at least an attitude scale could be constructed. An *a priori* scale can be constructed (exactly as for the degree of intellectual demand) which ranges between two extremes. It is relatively easy to say whether a given course is on average and on balance more involved or less involved with the application of knowledge to industrial, commercial, governmental, social and other prob-

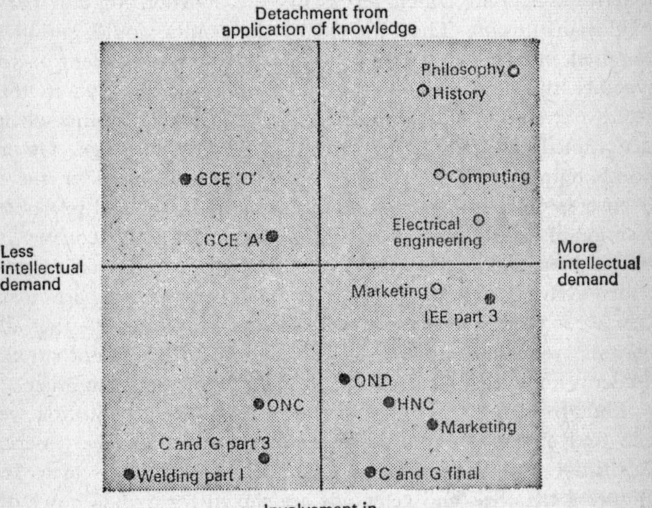

Figure 3 The courses are placed in the array on two scales which are arbitrary in that neither the zero nor the units of measurement, let alone the quantification of the latter, are determined. But they show a judgement (made as little subjective as possible by discussion) of the *relative* positions of these courses

lems than some other course. This does not mean that the difference is – at any rate at this stage – quantifiable. A course, for example, which had as its objective the personal and moral development of students would however on this scale rank very differently from a course in oxy-acetylene welding.

Given these two dimensions, we can look first at the array of courses within a given institution. In Figure 3 the lower part of the diagram contains a number of points which represent a judgement of the position of various courses in a technical college on the scales of intellectual demand and knowledge application. Thus an HNC is more demanding than an ONC or OND; a C and G final course is more oriented to application of knowledge than GCE 'O' and 'A' level courses. If each course in a college were plotted in this way, a scatter diagram for the whole institution would result. From this it is possible to determine a point which represents the 'location' of that particular institution. The centroid of the points would give the required indication; it is a matter of further judgement as to whether the points should be given weights according to the relative strengths of the courses. But the centroid point, when determined, will apply to that one technical college. Other points represent other colleges. As technical colleges differ, there is an area on the diagram which represents the overall probable location of technical colleges. Similar remarks apply to courses in universities, and in the upper right-hand corner a few university courses have been marked out. The difficulty with this particular exercise is the university convention – patently untrue – that all courses are equally intellectually demanding. This is not so; all students know that some courses are much tougher than others.

Thus from the array of courses within a given institution we can find an area on the diagram which represents the generic institution, and a point which is the centroid of this area. In Figure 4 the areas and centroids are shown for a wide range of institutions, and only the centroid for others. While the generic institutions differ in their position on the array, there are considerable overlaps between the areas representing the institutions collectively. Thus there are overlaps between girls' finishing schools and convents as much as there are between polytechnics and technological universities.

The diagram may perhaps enable us to understand better the relative roles of universities, polytechnics, research institutes, works training schools and so on. If we allow for the difference in intellectual demands in each type of organization, and additionally allow for differences in attitudes towards applications of knowledge in them, it is quickly evident that there is no single definition of the characteristics of any one type of organization.

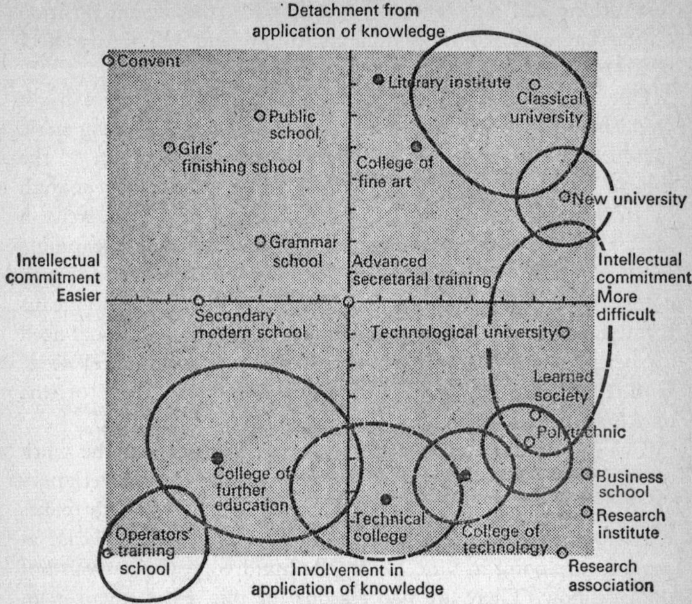

Figure 4 The same remarks concerning scales apply to this figure as to Figure 3. The judgement in this case is as to the relative positions of the generic institution on the array. There is considerable overlap in many if not most cases, and no doubt there will be disagreements on location and degree of overlap. Those shown may be agreeable or disagreeable to individuals for a wide variety of reasons

Any attempt at such a single-pointed definition can quickly be refuted by pointing to a practical case. Thus, for example, the School of Brewing at Birmingham can hardly be said to be divorced from the most immediate needs of industry! It is possible, that is, to point to work in various sectors which over-laps work in other sector or sectors. But overall the distinctions remain valid. Moreover, the diagram enables us to resolve con-tradictions about the various roles played by courses having the same title (I have in mind Law). A course in one university may be highly oriented to application of knowledge; a course in another may not. Similarly for courses in polytechnics. The differences between courses bearing the same title in different institutions will not, however, greatly affect the overall position on the diagram of an individual institution, and will hardly affect the typical institution's position at all.

One matter should now be abundantly clear; if need be, it could be put to some empirical test. The position of the generic polytechnic on the array is different from the position of the typical university. The test could be constructed easily enough by drawing for a typical polytechnic and typical university a scatter diagram of the courses they offer, weighting the points with numbers representing the number of students on each course. The final locations will differ, of course, but by no means through accident. The polytechnics are filling the vocational need of society, while the universities are catering for the ideal need; both functions are valid and necessary. Monitoring of the matching function is essential for stability of the system.

The question arises whether the areas representing the work of the universities and the polytechnics respectively overlap to an extent – greater than that shown in Figure 4 – which makes it irrelevant to distinguish them. This may well be the case at some future point in time, say in one hundred years, but it is not the case now. There are two reasons for this. First, there is an inherent difference between many degree courses offered in universities and those offered in polytechnics. The differences include the greater use of the sandwich principle, the increasing breakdown of traditional subject boundaries, more unconventional means of assessment, such as the use of project work, etc. So that on the diagram representing courses, the points for degrees in a university and a polytechnic may well be differently located, even if the degrees are ostensibly the same.

Second, there is much difference between the overall ranges of courses offered. In simple terms, universities will offer many more courses in humanities; they will offer more higher degrees; they will have less in the way of courses in business studies; and they will have no work involving higher technicians at all. The last point is crucial. The volume of higher technician work is potentially and actually very great, and the overall shape of the area representing polytechnics must therefore remain quite different from that of the universities.

Before leaving the array or structure diagram, there are two further points to be made. The first is the difference between the two concepts 'involvement in the application of knowledge' and 'matching and monitoring'. It is wrong to assume that anything involved in application of knowledge is matching, and anything not so involved is monitoring. Two examples may serve to illustrate the difference. First, a research association – say the Production Engineering Research Association – may be intimately concerned with the immediate application of knowledge to some industrial problem. It need not on this account be concerned with the future economy of the country and be involved in decisions about the educational opportunities to be provided, i.e. it need not be concerned with the matching function. No doubt if it were asked to make detailed forecasts it could do so, but this is another matter; it would then be carrying out a specific piece of research on which the matching decisions could in part be based.

The second example might relate to a convent, which can hardly be said to be concerned with the immediate application of knowledge; yet it would not in the generic case comment on social trends. No doubt its parent church would do so, but then a church has functions other than education.

The second point to be considered about the array of institutions is whether the criteria of detachment or involvement in the application of knowledge are relevant. To be specific, there are many left-wing staff and students who would consider that a study of, say, Marx or Marcuse is the most relevant item in the curriculum, and that study of present-day business techniques has no immediate application to the society that is about to arrive. Their criteria for the immediate application of knowledge would result in a somewhat different diagram, shown in outline in Figure 5. The study of present-day production systems, geared to the 'bourgeois capitalist' system, would be regarded as detached from the left-wing real world.

This difference in criteria of relevance is very similar to that adopted by Karl Mannheim's division of ideology into two kinds. The criteria of relevance used earlier correspond to the stability of the present and the remainder of the twentieth century. The criteria used by left-wing theorists are utopian, i.e. concerned with the ideology of revolt, of religious and political aspiration,

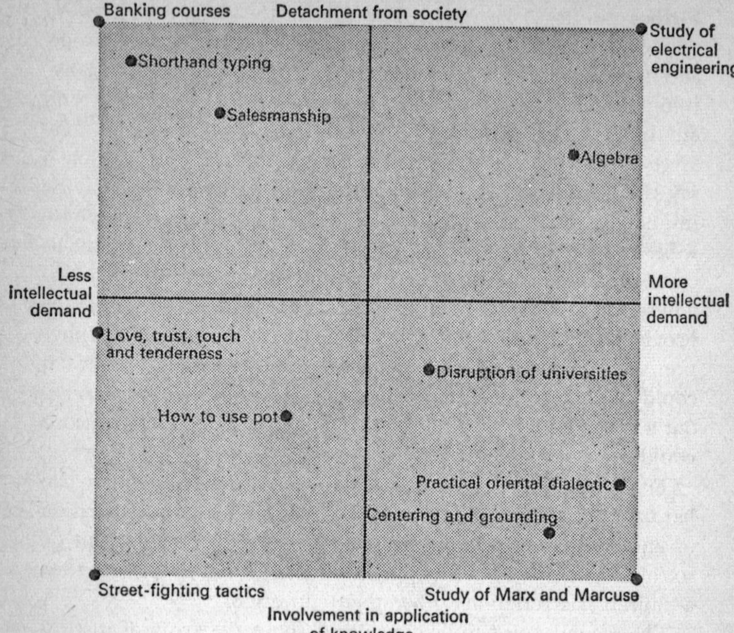

Figure 5 As before, courses are placed on scales which are arbitrary. The bases of judgements are however not Keynesian. In abstract terms this does not necessarily make them either more valid or invalid. Some examples of courses are taken from the 1968 prospectus of the Midpeninsular Free University, Stanford, California

and of messianic dreams of some romantic future. Students of Mannheim will no doubt recognize the identification with social groups. Even on this basis, the array of institutions would show clear differences between technical colleges, polytechnics and universities.

Degrees of freedom in polytechnics

The hierarchy-of-esteem argument put forward to decide the relative places of universities and polytechnics has another persuasive advocate in the relative degrees of freedom. Universities are free academically and controlled in resource by finance allocated mainly through the UGC. The kindest thing that can be said about the control of polytechnics, both individually and collectively, is that the system is decentralized and divergent. An unkind comment would be that it is chaotic; and in actual operation the system feels as though it is operating somewhere between the two extremes. Polytechnics, in common with other colleges in the public sector, are remarkable for the fact that they obtain necessary agreements for authority to proceed with their activities from a wide range of bodies. The ensuing confusion has been, perhaps unfairly, described as the last refuge of the entrepreneur where opportunities present themselves at no cost-risk.

The approvals are determined by a complex system, of which the following is no more than a bare outline. It includes:

Administrative approval of courses

Governing body and sub-committees
Local education authority and sub-committees
Regional advisory council and sub-committees
Regional staff inspector

Academic approval of courses

About 150 joint committees, examining bodies, institutions, universities, the CNAA, etc.

Approval of buildings

Governing body and sub-committees
Local education authority and sub-committees
Local authority and sub-committees
Department of Education and Science (several branches)

Approval of equipment

As for buildings. For items over £1,000 each item requires separate approval

Approval of staff

Governing body and sub-committees
Local education authority and sub-committees
Local authority and sub-committees (generally for non-teaching staff)
Department of Education and Science (in certain cases)

This is a system which *can* lead to chaos; that it has not done so frequently in the past is a tribute to the patience and hard work of the people involved. A college can simultaneously get approval and disapproval for a proposed course of action, e.g. agreement on staff but not on buildings, agreement to offer a course in administrative terms but refusal in academic terms. And so on.

The different types of control structure do, on occasion, exert mutually conflicting influences on each other and make life difficult for the administrators of the system. Even this is not intrinsically bad; administrators are, after all, paid to overcome such problems. The crucial effect is that the conflicting requirements of the many bodies which claim (sometimes on scant evidence) to be able to tell a college what it shall do, largely prevent it from developing any educational philosophy of its own. Save in a few exceptional cases, these complicated requirements negate the idea of a single philosophy for the institution as a whole.

The colleges from which the polytechnics sprang are accustomed to having a system imposed on them from the outside. In one sense, perhaps a rather shocking one, they *deserve* to have a system imposed. The colleges taken as a collective body are in fact disorganized, unpredictable and pluralistic in their interests. If, on the contrary, they were highly organized, predictable in response, and unitary in their views, they would be in a much better position to comment on and influence the different types of control structure which are imposed on them. This is in accordance with the general proposition in social science that the more highly differentiated and the less stable the general social setting is, the less prominent it will be. The converse is also true. The very flexibility of the college system, i.e. its adaptibility to many sorts and changes of needs, means that its internal procedures are not considered important and its teaching methods are not prominent in the discussions on what is to be done. Thus, if an external validating body says: offer courses on a unit system (e.g. as the recommendations of the Haslegrave Report), a college will offer courses on a unit system. If another validating body comes along and says: your courses must be fully integrated and all parts of it must be demonstrably linked with all other parts (as with the CNAA, for example), then the college will set to and design, or try to design, an integrated course. This is despite the fact that the two philosophies are quite different in educational terms! Under these conditions what hope is there for an institution to develop a course philosophy of its own? In fact there are not many colleges which have one. This is reflected in much of the teaching that goes on. It is invariably competent and thorough, given the constraints. The staff in colleges, with a great deal of enthusiasm and efficiency, *operate a system that has been designed by some outside body.* That is, the great majority of teachers in the public sector of further and higher education are compelled, despite their abilities, to perform the function of technicians. They should of course be allowed to operate as technologists of education and design their own systems, but until there is some means of changing the external multiple-control structure this is unlikely to happen.

The reason for describing the operation of the colleges is that the polytechnics have emerged from the college structure. At the time of writing they are gradually diverging from the other senior colleges in the public sector. There are a few exceptions where the change is much faster and there is far less resemblance to their antecedents.

The decision structure for the polytechnics is in some ways very similar to the decision structure for colleges; the main change is that the powers of the LEA, and especially reference of matters to its sub-committees, is reduced. Effective powers of the governing bodies are increased. But the overall problem of multiple external control remains. The major weakness at the moment in the strategy of polytechnic development is that the new structure has become trapped in the assumptions of the existing structure. Care needs to be taken lest the new one should become impotent. It is thus of great importance to polytechnics that they should obtain a rationalization of multiple external control. This can be attempted, it is true, by seeking abolition of various controls. But this is not a realistic procedure in the present political climate. A more practical method would be for polytechnics to assume a collective responsibility for academic validation of all courses they offer. Validation would be internal, with external assessment. Such procedures are at least logical, in that institutions which have the academic capability to offer Ph.D.s, Master's degrees and Honours degrees presumably have the capability of dealing with academic aspects of other courses.

As we have seen, it is probably true that the organizational structure of a college or polytechnic reflects its system of educational beliefs. Another assumption of the system from which the polytechnics emerged was that the general means of education should continue on the same basis as hitherto. This implies a huge amount of data-centred instruction based principally on ingestion and regurgitation of information. Information is validated by some committee outside the student, and then has to be validated again inside the student. The first process, which occupies the time of a very large number of academic committees, is called syllabus or curriculum construction; the second is called examination. This is hardly an extreme statement if it is recollected that few, if any, syllabuses state in any form what a student should be able to do at the end of the course; they state what he should know. They state in some cases what he should understand, but fail to specify what he must do in order to demonstrate that understanding. There is no specification of attitudes.

Most important, the relation of the curriculum to the normal experience-centred learning that goes on throughout life is not considered to any extent; yet experience-centred learning is the norm in most activities other than the formal educational system. The organizational structure required for this sort of learning is not yet available. The polytechnics have within the next few years the opportunity, and I believe the duty, to try to evolve alternative forms of undergraduate education which would be unacceptable in the university tradition. Direction of intellectual effort to alternative areas of knowledge and the demonstration of the greater application and relevance to current problems are part of the answer, but do not go anything like far enough. The widespread student concern over the irrelevance of syllabuses is directed only in part to the subject content. It is also directed against the means of subject-content transmission and the underlying hypothesis that problems can be studied in a worthwhile way only in an intellectual context (the university hypothesis). Thoughtful students are asking for a re-styling of the curriculum so that it involves some elements of human life that are intuitive and expressive rather than merely intellectual. Students are in part expressing a wish to be involved in the real world of action and opportunity; they do not yet know about frustration, disappointment and fear. But so great is the pressure towards higher education as a certifying agency that many students, perhaps justifiably, will not accept the direct challenge to go untutored into the world.

The need that polytechnics could fulfil is to devise a new form of higher education in which the adult over eighteen can affiliate to the polytechnic for study, while at the same time being involved in actualities. The means of achieving this can be worked out easily enough if the objectives are clear; the students may well obtain a qualification of some kind, but this would be regarded as a secondary matter by all concerned. What matters primarily is that the student should be able to use his actual experience as a framework for learning *outside* the normal lecture, seminar and tutorial system, with the laboratory as an adjunct in many cases.

It is not suggested that this form of education is apt for all students and all disciplines or activities, especially at first. There may well be only a small minority of students who would wish to commit themselves to such an unusual form of study. This may seem to be a contradiction in the expressed needs of students, but as is well known there are many students who express a conflicting view about the appropriateness (or lack of appropriateness) of formal education on the one hand, and their determination to succeed within it on the other. It may be useful to illustrate the concept briefly for engineering, an area of study now commonly undertaken in both universities and polytechnics.

In engineering the most common assumption is that there is a great deal of specific knowledge that the engineer requires before he can be expected to engage in any kind of practice at all. The discipline is 'hard boned' and is often oriented heavily towards engineering science and research. There are a number of alternative approaches being considered, but these are as yet in very early stages of development. For this reason, the engineer needs to spend several years in ingesting information before he can in any way apply it. One unfortunate result of this system is that the student is for a very long time unable to see any kind of relevance of the study he undertakes to the realities of engineering as he knows of them by direct or vicarious experience. This applies even to sandwich courses in the earlier parts of the course. It also means that any innovative or entrepreneurial qualities which the student may have atrophy through lack of use and often from direct discouragement.

Suppose that instead of entering college after leaving school the prospective student entered industry as a special kind of trainee. As he began to work, he would find that there were many things that he did not know which he needed to know in order better to carry out his tasks in relation to his purposes. It is relatively simple to think of a system of education which could supply this motivated student with the information, concepts and skills he required; one has only to mention data banks, computers, programmed learning, guided reading, etc. Access to this system could be through a mechanism similar to the education bank now being considered in Scandinavia, in which each qualified student would have the right to a given amount of instruction, without any cost, in recognized institutions. This education bank could be drawn on at any time in a person's life. As will be realized, this type of education is not sandwich, nor some form of day release following a given syllabus for a given qualification; it is rather a partial reversion to the medieval idea that apprentice scholars go to sit at the feet of a teacher whom they want to hear. That, in the modern context, could be arranged; the teacher may of course use a range of methods other than verbal communication to carry out his role.

Peter Venables
Expansion and Overlap of Functions

To establish an array of institutions, each uniquely characterized in its functions, and for each of which a uniquely characterized group of students can be selected annually with absolute accuracy, is a task fortunately incapable of achievement; but it is the unspoken underlying ideal assumption of much discussion about the planning of institutions and their relationships. Indeed, it is the most charitable explanation of the aggressive, overcompensating publicity attendant on the creation of seven new universities, the transformation of the colleges of advanced technology into technological universities, and currently on the emergence of the polytechnics from the regional colleges of technology and other vocational institutions. As for the present range of institutions (chapter 3), there is a varying and sometimes quite substantial overlap of functions between them. None of the new, transformed or newly emergent institutions is uniquely determined, whatever its protagonists may have claimed,[1] and this is really more advantageous for the students and for the body politic. Selection with absolute accuracy is impossible, individual changes of interests and motivations are not predictable, and occupational changes and choices are not strictly determinable. Planned changes in the educational system take years to become fully effective, and by that time the circumstances for which they were made have altered, even quite radically. Planning must therefore be broad and flexible, and future needs cannot be met by creating some allegedly unique institution – whether 'free' or not – that will remain so thereafter.

Hitherto, institutions of higher and further education have proved capable of constructive changes, of modifying established

1. The present author wryly admits to doing his bit at the time: the gentle art of overstatement is a curious fact of public advocacy and exposition, especially when resources are scarce, and one which is apt to become more rigorous and less scrupulous under the influence of modern mass media.

purposes and embracing new ones effectively, and occasionally of creating additional institutions as by-products of the process. In what follows this modification of existing institutions is assumed to be the most efficient and flexible basis for the expansion required by 1980; before new institutions are considered the question of the pressure of numbers, and of the belief that essential educational innovations cannot otherwise be secured, will need to be very critically examined.

The university part of the system

Existing and adjacent available sites should be used to the maximum capacity, and enrolments increased from the figure of about 220,000 students in 1969–70 to about 450,000 in 1980. The provisional UGC target for the end of the 1972–7 quinquennium is 330,000, and a figure of about 480,000 appears probable for the end of the next quinquennium – a shortfall of about 30,000 which might perhaps justify the creation of additional universities. Arguments of geography and particular industries; of beautiful environments and splendid heritage; of cultural and economic regeneration; of unique support and total involvement – all these no doubt will be paraded and stressed again, with the same old fervour and alleged realism, as if twenty-two additional universities had not already been created in a single decade. On these grounds, probable and unlikely claims may be advanced for Stamford, Teesside, Wolverhampton, Hereford (Cathedral), Melrose (Abbey), Llandrindod (Wells) and Hebrides (Outer). It is difficult not to be sceptical, and wonder why the addition of 40,000 students, i.e. 10 per cent of the total, spread among forty-six existing universities should be so profoundly difficult as to justify yet another group of new universities being created; the more so, considering what can yet reasonably be done in improving traditional practices. For example, staff–student ratios should be revised, taking advantage of any aspects of modern educational technology which save staff effort. Training should be provided for new staff and recurrent refresher courses for established staff. Improvements could also result from establishing new balances of practical laboratory work to theoretical studies in undergraduate courses, by readjustments of the working day and year, by deferring specialization to later years, and by increasing the proportion of common or combined courses. The proportion of postgraduate courses should be much increased – especially post-experience courses for Master's degrees – on a part-time or block-release basis, and made financially self-supporting as far as possible with grants from the industrial training boards, or other appropriate bodies.

The polytechnic part of the system

The polytechnics are not uniquely characterized institutions, as their origins in differing institutions make plain. They are hybrid institutions, and if, as all would hope (though for different reasons and purposes), they are successful in their diverse functions, they will indeed be fertile hybrids. In considering their functions we need to bear in mind the structure and level of work shown in Table 12, the changes which took place in the colleges of advanced technology on becoming technological universities, and the changes which have taken place in the universities generally in recent years. On this basis the future profiles of these three groups may be broadly shown (Table 12).

It would be useful to be able to quantify the profile for polytechnics as shown in Table 12 at present, and to estimate the corresponding figures for 1980, but many considerations prevent this. Polytechnics have not all been designated (p. 54), and those which are have not had time to reorganize and develop significantly some of the functions indicated. As for 1980, the biggest uncertainty in Table 12 is not so much the range of functions, as the nature of the courses to be provided. In quantitative terms this is most important with undergraduate and sub-degree courses. Present indications are that undergraduate courses in science and technology are somewhat overprovided for in the universities, and laboratories and special equipment should therefore not be provided for additionally on an extensive scale in the polytechnics. There is, and for a long time likely to be, a much greater demand for courses in arts and social sciences, and this should be shared in the expansion of the universities, the polytechnics and, last but certainly not least, the colleges of education. The polytechnics are already developing these courses, and some have established departments of education, but if this became very substantial, the 'technic' would decline relative to

Table 12
Work Profiles

Range of work	Polytechnics	Technological universities	Other universities
Postgraduate work			
Research: Ph.D. and beyond			
Fundamental		X	XXX
Applied*	X	XXX	X(X)
Courses: Master's degrees			
Full-time		X	XX
Sandwich†	X	XXX	X
Part-time	XX	XX	X
Courses: Diploma, etc.			
Professional	XXX	XX	X
Short refresher*	XX	XXX	XX(X)
Undergraduate work			
Honours degrees			
Full-time	X	X	XXX
Sandwich†	XXX	XXX	(X)
Part-time	XX	X	
Pass degrees**	XXX	X	X
Sub-degree courses			
2- and 3-year diploma courses††	XXX		
Advanced technicians	XX		
Advanced craft	X		

X indicates some commitment.
XX indicates substantial commitment.
XXX indicates very strong commitment.
 *For universities with strong technological and science departments XX would be more accurate, and in a few cases XXX would be justified.

the rest, and the 'poly' would in reality become British 'liberal science colleges' (as compared with some colleges of education becoming 'liberal arts colleges'). These after all may provide a far better educational environment for many students than the more narrowly based polytechnics. By an extensive provision of combined honours/pass degree/diploma courses, for students entering with GCE 'A' level science and arts subjects, and ONC (or whatever), the routes could be opened to students, or kept open for them, and this would powerfully offset too early a specialization at 'Q' and 'F' (or whatever) levels. At the same time, however, we must emphasize that the most desirable change in further education is to convert part-time day-release courses into sandwich courses and substantial block-release courses, and this would transform the general situation and justify a ranking of XXX for sub-degree courses as a whole for polytechnics.

The polytechnics' most important function is teaching, and it would be absurdly uneconomical in terms of facilities and teaching resources were they to attempt any substantial development of research alongside the technological departments

---

† Quite a few examples exist of universities establishing sandwich courses, or courses on the same principle, involving professional training within the overall period of education prior to qualification (i.e. new ones in addition to medical courses, which are the longest established sandwich courses of all).

** It is assumed that pass-degree courses will serve two main purposes in polytechnics : as slightly upgraded Higher National Diploma courses in specialist disciplines, and as a useful sorting-out stage for students; and that thus they will be mainly generalist in character, e.g. common courses or combined subject courses, and should offer a real opportunity for experiment in establishing a credit system in this country. Pass-degree courses or options exist in quite a number of unversities, but the problem is to establish them as ends in themselves, so that they are not regarded as 'failed honours' courses – to afford to the students, in fact, what Spurr describes as 'non-invidious choices' (p. 98).

†† Sub-degree diploma courses will provide for limited objectives for specific skills prior to entry to employment, and for reorientation towards new objectives, e.g. craft students who show promise of becoming technicians and possibly professional technologists. They would thus provide the modern more ample equivalent of the former arduous part-time system. (It is assumed that the main objectives of the Haslegrave Report of the Committee on Technician Courses and Examinations, 1969, will be established.)

of universities and the technological universities. Their post-graduate contribution should be largely through courses for professional requirements and updating courses, especially part-time ones, together with a much smaller volume of specialist courses for Master's degrees. Otherwise their students should proceed, across the boundaries of the binary system (if that system persists), to undertake research and postgraduate studies in the universities. It does not suffice to assert that this view is merely the rationalized dog-in-a-manger attitude of the ex-CATs, now securely chartered as technological universities.

If that change were a good thing for eight institutions, it will not bear repetition in foreseeable circumstances for another thirty-one. There are simply not the resources, and they are not likely to exist within several decades, if ever, for seventy-seven university-level institutions to exercise efficiently the functions set out in Table 12; nor is it likely to happen even on the basis, as would be the natural but untoward consequence, of the shedding of all sub-degree courses. The thirty-one polytechnics are by no means so homogeneous a group of institutions, especially in standards, as were the former ten colleges of advanced technology. Moreover, those who were responsible for ensuring the successful transition of the colleges to university status, academic staff and administrative alike, know from first-hand experience the onerous nature of the tasks which await the leading polytechnics, let alone those for the remainder. Designation ensures nothing of itself, and is but the formal condition of entry to a long and arduous struggle to raise and maintain standards which are the hallmark of academic work. This is an inescapable fact of life for higher academic institutions, no matter what the nature and variety of their particular functions might be. Moreover if non-invidious choices are to be created and maintained for students between institutions and courses, then the polytechnics must have the opportunity (as distinct from an absolute assurance) of reaching fully accredited and chartered status, to preserve their own orientation and purposes on their own terms (see pp. 97–8).

The overlapping of functions between institutions is not confined to those in Table 12; it occurs also between polytechnics and area colleges, colleges of technology, art and commerce respectively. The overlapping is from undergraduate and professional work downwards through sub-degree courses, while the other (non-poly) institutions have varying amounts, often substantial, of lower-level technician craft, and general-education courses. A major difference between the American and British systems is the important part played by the community colleges and liberal arts colleges.[1] The growing change in our society and economy, following substantially on the American pattern, does strongly indicate the emergence of comparable institutions in the United Kingdom; not, however, by specially created models, but by the modification of existing institutions on the lines suggested (p. 94).

The colleges of education

The authors of this book know the colleges from the outside, and must defer to those who are concerned with teacher training, and to experienced teachers in the schools, in discussing future policy. Yet there are some general observations which can properly be made, having regard to the growing public discussion of this sector of higher education. Three aspects certainly require consideration in the light of certain parts of this book – the emergence of a graduate profession, the need to add generalist functions to specialist institutions, and the fact that a single or narrow vocational purpose is no longer a sufficient justification for an institution of higher education (p. 95). The colleges have very little overlap of function with other institutions though universities have departments of education providing mostly one-year postgraduate diploma courses in education, and polytechnics have recently begun to establish departments of education with undergraduate courses.

The future of the colleges is inextricably bound up with the major question of establishing a graduate teaching profession, instead of simply increasing slowly the supply of graduates through the B.Ed. degree over decades to come. Otherwise the profession will lose out in the fast-growing competition for ability: a non-graduate profession, educated largely in single-

1. E. Alden Dunham, *Colleges of the Forgotten Americans*, Carnegie Commission on Higher Education, McGraw-Hill, 1969.

purpose institutions, cut off from the wide range of other students and activities, will fail to attract its quota of able students and – as present trends already indicate – predestined solitary grooves may cease to attract at all. Whether we like it or not, in the Era of Consent this will be the result of the inevitable decline in occupational determinism – whether that is feudal, parental, economic, geographical, political or religious in origin.

The arguments rest on other grounds besides that of the need for able teachers, but can only be very briefly summarized here.[1] If we get rid of the idea that nursery- and primary-school teachers are mainly and merely 'child-minders', of a lower status than secondary-school teachers, and ask what qualities and abilities teachers in all types of school ought to have, it is difficult to remain satisfied with the assumption that they should be of sub-graduate level. The profession needs people with a deep understanding of the development of personality, of human needs generally, of the nature of an increasingly complex society, and with a capacity and commitment actively to sustain 'values' within that society – humane, cultural, religious and philosophic. Recruitment from those who fail to get into a university course does not seem the best way to secure these qualities, and the increased number of qualified entrants in the 1970s affords a belated opportunity for making teaching in England and Wales a fully graduate profession.

A graduate profession of teaching would have a great deal in common with the personal service professions also emerging towards full graduate status, and training for these would be the concern of the multi-purpose institutions which the colleges of education should become. These include youth workers, community workers, and social workers involved in welfare work, mental welfare, personnel departments, probation work and child care. The degree courses would have common-core studies comprising human development – biological, physiological, norms of development; psychology and psycho-dynamics; development of skills in human relationships by group-discussion methods; recognition of serious mental and emotional troubles, and of

1. See P. Venables, 'Competitors for ability, and a graduate profession', *Education for Teaching*, December 1970.

physical difficulties; and introductory social studies. Special studies would include as relevant: academic studies; teaching methods and other professional skills; management studies; law; and social and educational history. With such studies, and with strong courses in English, history and some languages, the colleges would be transformed into liberal arts colleges (in which nevertheless provision for the need for numeracy and science is not an afterthought). They would thus provide a far wider educational environment for teachers than exists in most colleges now.

The reason for having single-vocation institutions is believed to be that the Department of Education and Science thus gains a precise and delicate control over the numbers entering the profession. If there were multi-purpose colleges, presumably too many would transfer out of the teaching courses, and the necessary supply for the schools would not be maintained. This amounts to saying that some who want to transfer (and no doubt some who ought to do so) are being forced into teaching against their will. This implies a curious lack of confidence in the normal methods of securing sufficient recruits for a profession, namely, satisfactory salaries and conditions of service.

This fear is the major inhibiting obstacle to the colleges becoming truly multi-purpose graduate institutions, but changes similar to those proposed for the colleges have been taking place in the United States. E. Alden Dunham (in *Colleges of the Forgotten Americans*) states:

It does not appear to be the case that the supply of teachers is shrinking as institutions become more multi-purpose in nature. The percentage of graduating seniors prepared to enter teaching does go down – now about 62 per cent in state colleges – but in absolute numbers teaching production goes up because of vastly increasing enrolment.

The view is taken that a college has

no more of an obligation to turn out teachers for the public schools than it has to provide sufficient nurses or engineers. It is left to these fields to compete for and attract people, implying that the way to maintain the supply of teachers, for example, is to make the teaching profession an attractive one. And that is someone else's business. ...

This view is becoming common in state after state, as the former state teachers' colleges become multi-purpose and come out from under the control of the state departments of education.

The British parallels are the controversies about Burnham salaries and conditions of service, and about the administration and governance of the colleges of education by local education authorities.

No uniform expansion across the board will be possible for the colleges of education because of their varied size and location, but the majority could be expanded to become multi-purpose institutions. However, the solutions will depend on two main factors – the realistic attainment of a graduate profession, and the relations which might be established with other institutions. A graduate profession will not be achieved by the development of the B.Ed. degree; moreover, the present system by which a small proportion of students go on to the B.Ed. course is not viable. The efforts made by the colleges to enhance their status by becoming recognized for the degree, under regulations prescribed by the university concerned, has produced the same serious defects of fragmentation which the Department of Education and Science (following the Pilkington recommendation) has been trying to remedy in further-education colleges. Thus, if a college of nine hundred students has an annual entry of three hundred, and is able to add B.Ed. studies with an intake of 15 per cent of each annual group, this will provide forty-five B.Ed. students to spread over some ten to fifteen subjects. Under these circumstances a 'large' subject-group will be seven or eight (except in education, perhaps taken by all forty-five): some subjects, particularly in science, will have only one or two students per college per year. Whatever benefits this may bring in individual tuition, it is plainly nonsense to provide advanced laboratory facilities and teachers capable of advanced work for such small groups.

Relationships with other institutions would depend on geography and transport, on their particular background and cognate studies. Some could become part of federated institutions by combining with other colleges, with polytechnics or with universities, but the major ones should be enabled to become chartered institutions in their own right. With all these possibilities, and the additional range of purposes and disciplines, a total of 250,000 students would not be excessive.[1]

The accreditation of institutions

For the reasons stated in chapter 4 (pp. 97–8), this is regarded as an integral part of a balanced expansion, by which conforming influences are to be kept in check, and a healthy diversity of excellent institutions is secured. As the National Council for Technological Awards was important to the early growth and attainments of the colleges of advanced technology, and as the CNAA is proving likewise for the polytechnics, so will the CNAA – if need be with suitably modified powers, or some other body of the requisite standing – be essential for the emergence and recognition of excellence in the variety of institutions now proposed.

The expansion of adult education

This is not directly part of the expansion of tertiary education necessary to cope with the onrush of qualified entrants from the schools, but it is of vital importance in creating the most advantageous context in which that expansion should take place. Despite the growth in recent years (p. 48), a much greater and imaginative provision of adult education is essential to reduce the incubus of adult ignorance, inertia and indifference against which so much educational development has to struggle. Against this long continuing background of struggle and devoted effort, two recent events are particularly significant.

The first is the establishment in February 1969 of the Committee on Adult Education (Chairman, Sir Lionel Russell) to consider the needs and development of the great range of non-vocational adult education in this country, through voluntary and statutory and responsible bodies (p. 47). Its report and recommendations will be awaited with exceptional interest, and present resources and allocations of finance must be substantially increased if progress is to be at least commensurate with the urgent needs already evident.

1. Compare 220,000 in the 1970 ATCDE Report, *A Policy for Colleges of Education*, which is not very specific about cognate professions, nor fully aware of new developments such as those which should follow the Seebohm Report.

The second event is the establishment of the Open University. It originated as a proposal to establish a University of the Air, and owed a great deal to the initiative of Harold Wilson, and to the continuing interest of Miss Jennie Lee, but, as was understood by all concerned, it is in no sense a party political institution.[1] The University was established by procedures very similar to those which obtained for all the new universities of recent years. A Planning Committee was appointed by the Secretary of State for Education and Science in September 1967 'To work out a comprehensive plan for an Open University, as outlined in the White Paper of February 1966, *A University of the Air*, and to prepare a draft Charter and Statutes'. The Committee reported in January 1969,[2] the charter was granted in May 1969, and presented in the rooms of the Royal Society in July 1969.

The change in name was significant. In the early years broadcasting will play a central role, and in 1971 each of the four foundation courses will have one TV programme (on BBC-2), and one radio programme (on UHF) each week; further programmes will be developed in later years. But from the start broadcasting will be only one of the methods used; others will be correspondence, programmed teaching materials, and many sorts of audio-visual technique. Broadcasting may be expected to decline in importance as the technology of videotape recording and reproducing develops over the next few years. Recorded programmes, on loan as books from libraries, studied at home and at viewing centres arranged by the University, will thus liberate times of study from broadcasting timetable necessities. No less important is that, from the start, the content and progress of all the methods used will be related and planned as a whole. Altogether, this will constitute the modern equivalent of the revolution in learning and access to knowledge brought about by Caxton's Press. An important side-effect is likely to be the impact of the University's work on that of other educational institutions, and perhaps most in the clarity and effectiveness of

1. The first officers were: Chancellor, Lord Crowther; Pro-Chancellor and Chairman of Council, Sir Peter Venables; Vice-Chancellor, Dr W. L. M. Perry; Treasurer, Sir Paul Chambers.
2. *The Open University*, HMSO, 1969.

teaching. Another may well be in the sales of its courses and materials, both at home and abroad.

Starting in 1971, the University will have four foundation courses: in the Arts, the Social Sciences, the Natural Sciences and Mathematics; and a fifth in Technology will start in 1972, all leading to a B.A. degree. As with all other new universities, including the technological ones, the University under its charter has an academic advisory committee, to help establish academic standards and procedures over its first five years or so of development. There are no examination entrance requirements to the foundation courses, but no one may proceed to the second-, third-, and fourth-year courses without successfully passing the previous stages. Graduation will be by the accumulation of 'credits', one for each course, on certain conditions for a first and subsequently for an honours degree. As the University becomes established, postgraduate updating refresher courses will be developed on various patterns as well as more traditional courses and research adapted to the conditions of the University, and leading by credits where suitable to higher degrees. In addition, research is already being developed into the subjects of study and the academic interests of staff, but also directed to analysing and improving the University's own work – content of courses, methodology, educational technology, the learning responses of students and so on.

The University has set up twelve regional offices and 250 study centres altogether in England, Wales and Scotland, so that as few students as possible will be out of reach of one. Personal contact will be fostered by each student having an allocated counsellor at a study centre, a correspondence tutor and, wherever possible, a course tutor. In addition a residential summer school of at least one week forms an essential part of each course. The first main buildings of the University at Milton Keynes were opened by Earl Mountbatten in May 1969. By September 1969 full-time academic staff numbered 112, with 120 in administration, and 298 other staff, including specialists in many new technologies and skills required.

The planning committee was naturally concerned to assess the potential number of students likely to apply to the University, and made a broad comparison in terms of the proportion of the eighteen-year-old group entering full-time higher education at the beginning and end of the last three decades, and when the Robbins targets are reached (they are likely to be exceeded by at least 40 per cent – see chapter 2). The committee stated that:

Without doubt there has been a substantial, though slowly diminishing proportion of people able enough to enter higher education who were born too soon to reap the benefits of increasing educational opportunity. If the Robbins Report targets had applied retrospectively over the last three decades, the total number concerned could hardly be less than one million. It is not to be supposed that, of these, the majority would be both able and willing to undertake study after a gap of years, but perhaps 10 per cent (at least 100,000) might.

This first estimate was compared with the results of some pilot research investigations, and consideration was given to the rising standards required by professions over the three decades. For example, in the teaching profession there were 240,000 certificated non-graduate teachers in England and Wales and some 15,000 in Scotland (i.e. about 25,000 from this source alone).

If this major task of providing a second chance, or rather a first but later chance, for many would-be students were adequately dealt with, there would still be a serious ongoing problem. Social inequalities will not suddenly vanish, nor will all individuals suddenly and certainly mature at the same age in the same environment. Furthermore, various subjects and issues may not become meaningful or urgent until later on in adult life, which motivated students would then pursue – provided the facilities are available. Such subjects and issues are not only the vocational and professional ones, but concern the citizen as such, his politics, religion, philosophy, his interest in the arts, and other aspects of his own personal fulfilment.

Against all these considerations, we may note that enrolments for the first foundation courses, which closed on 9 August 1970, had by then reached 42,821 in number, of which less than 2 per cent were subsequently deemed to be unsatisfactory candidates. The government confirmed in August that finance would be provided for the planned first-year intake of 25,000 (equal to 30,000 course places) in January 1971, and invitations to the selected students were sent out in August 1970. The quotas of course places offered were 7,000 each in Mathematics and Science and 8,000 in Arts and Social Sciences. The composition of the application is of especial interest, not least in influencing the 'mix' of the 25,000 accepted. The geographical distribution was in fairly close accord with that of population in the regions, but the occupational distribution as compared with the Registrar-General's classification showed some sharp discrepancies. Those most discussed in the Press have been the high proportion of teachers and the low proportion of the working classes and lower-income groups as compared with the nation as a whole, but neither is surprising or unexpected. Teachers are well informed, and most likely to hear early of the establishment of the University; they have habits of study, and are also particularly interested in the opportunity to gain graduate status. It is a truism, so persistently ignored, that education generates a desire for more education, as witness the growth of further and higher education in the years following each raising of the school-leaving age; and the importance of parental education for the future of the offspring is shown in the Robbins Report. The other side is simply that years of lack of opportunity, of cumulative social disadvantage and unawareness, entail an atrophy which does not vanish when new opportunities are suddenly presented. The same state applies to the continuing effect of the lack of educational opportunities for women, who comprise less than one third of the applicants. The conclusion is not that the teachers should be further restricted in their opportunities or that the unskilled classes should be left in their unawareness, but that the University (and the community generally) must do far more to make its work more widely and effectively known to all classes of the community.

This is wholly in accord with the charter of the Open University, which states that its objects

shall be the advancement and dissemination of learning and knowledge by teaching and research by a diversity of means such as broadcasting and technological devices appropriate to higher education, by correspondence tuition, residential courses and seminars and in other relevant ways, and shall be to provide education of university and professional standards for its students and to *promote the educational well-being of the community generally* [author's italics].

As part of this wider context it has been suggested that, contrary to the firm recommendation of the planning committee, the scope of the University's work should be changed to include students aged eighteen to twenty-one years, and thus help to reduce the prospective lack of places for students in higher education as a whole, especially from 1975 onwards. As a responsible and responsive institution the Open University will wish to examine the feasibility of the proposal by suitable pilot experiments, preferably in cooperation with other institutions; and to do this in relation both to the needs and performance of students of this age range, and to the resources and proportion of effort which may be directed in this way. To put the latter point sharply, if the shortfall of student places were 60,000 per annum (at least) and the Open University were expected to take 20,000 per annum (at least) out of its present (unassured) intake of 25,000 per annum *without additional resources*, then its primary fuction would have been sacrificed. It is encouraging that powerful educational bodies have been quick to sense these particular dangers to the Open University. At the same time they have been sceptical about the educational suitability of these courses and methods for this age group assumed primarily on the grounds (whether explicit or not) of reduced cost per student-place. This assumption may unfortunately be reinforced in some quarters by another about the (alleged) advantages of 'beneficial employment'.

The educational wellbeing of the community is indispensable to the Era of Consent, and not only the Open University, but all the foregoing proposals and considerations must be critically appraised as to the way in which they will help to bring this about.

The administration of tertiary education

In this chapter the trend towards overlapping functions in more broadly based institutions as the best basis for expansion has been considered, but there remains a sharp contrast between a spectrum of broadly based tertiary institutions with overlapping functions and a binary system of national administration.

The binary system, while understandable in origin, encourages anomalies and fosters vestigial remains which no longer serve a useful purpose. The following examples will suffice : the granting of charters with degree-granting powers to a non-university body, and to non-university colleges; the financing of these colleges and of the Open University by direct grant from the DES and not through the UGC; the impossibility, as the profiles in Table 12 show, of making any absolute distinction between institutions of higher education and those offering higher education within the further-education sector; the disparate conditions of governance, administration, and conditions of service through this range of institutions; the necessity of related planning, especially of capital investment, to cover all the sectors of tertiary education as a whole; the need to secure the interrelatedness of institutions and courses – all these facts and considerations point to a unified system of administration of higher and tertiary education. This will entail acute problems and painful reappraisals as to national and local systems of administration and finance, the nature of institutions, and as to the rate of change commensurate with the best interests of all concerned, and not least of the generations of students involved. Evolution, revolution or plastic surgery – that is the question (see chapter 9).

One important consideration, now timely because of the recent turn of events, is the future relationship of the British system with higher education in Europe. A unified national system will help to establish good effective relationships, provided it is more flexible than hitherto, and that it both secures the conditions of excellence and provides (so belatedly) mass education at tertiary level. These are the two main concerns underlying the proposals made in this chapter. The system must provide interdependence and good relationships between its own institutions as an essential part of a wider context.

It will be a great disappointment for everybody if, ten years from now, it is not possible for a would-be student from (say) Manchester to sign up as if by right for a university course at Nancy or Munich, and if graduates from Rome cannot with equal ease take Ph.D. degrees at Birmingham (*Nature*, 27 June 1970).

That such considerations will not be limited to university courses is already evident in adult education, in the European prize contests for apprentices, and in the start made in providing periods of industrial training in European firms as part of sandwich courses.

Chapter Seven
Alternative Lines of Advance

In practical terms, then, what is to be done – given the existing
structure (outlined in chapter 3) and the requirements of the
expansion estimated in chapter 2? The alternative possibilities
are here set out. George Brosan wants a Polytechnics Grants
Committee, in parallel to the University Grants Committee,
and sees an opportunity for at least limited cooperation between
separate, but similarly grant-aided, sectors. Charles Carter sees
no chance of such a system providing economy or good planning,
nor does he think that the universities and the public-sector
colleges would enjoy 'parity of esteem'. He therefore sees the only
way forward as the establishment of regional or local federations
of institutions of higher education, all grant-aided by a central
grants committee. This would in turn involve setting aside the
present forms of University Charter. Peter Venables, while
sympathetic to the unification of the binary system, thinks this
goes too rapidly for political feasibility. He looks to a period of
fifteen years during which parallel university and public-sector
grants committees, with overlapping membership, would work
closely together, in the hope that the objective of a single central
committee would then be reached. He would also like to see a
system of accreditation, enabling institutions to evolve and attain
chartered independence, continuing as institutions in their own
right and kind, and not to be regarded as embryonic universities –
though in some areas a federation (such as Charles Carter
proposed) might be a possible and sensible solution.

George Brosan
Transbinary Cooperation

What then of cooperation across the two parts of the binary system? How does this work out under the concept of 'separate but equal' in a kind of higher-education apartheid?

First it must be said that the concept of 'separate but equal' is deeply repugnant to a very wide range of people. The Robbins precept was to the effect that institutions carrying out the same function should be given the same status and the same designation. This was the basis of the transmogrification of the CATs; and whether or not the CATs were carrying out the same task as the universities prior to their designation, they are increasingly doing so now. If then, the argument goes, the polytechnics are carrying out a function which is elsewhere carried out by the universities, they too should become universities.

I disagree. To begin with, the polytechnics are not carrying out the same role as the universities. Again, going on the experience of the CATs, nothing would make the polytechnics change their function quicker than absorption in the university system.

Second, there is every reason (except one) for commonsense arrangements of sharing expensive apparatus, equipment, facilities, amenities and the like. If something is available for general use in the community, it should be used to the full. Several such arrangements exist. It is difficult to take this idea seriously, however, for the one reason that I mentioned – explicitly, that the trade is all one way. The universities are so much better equipped, have so much more in the way of allowances, student amenities and so on that, in practice (save a few quite special cases), they are giving much to the polytechnics and getting little or nothing in return. This is generous of the universities and is widely acknowledged as such, but a form of association based on what too easily takes the form of patronage is not a basis for fruitful interchange nor long-term goodwill.

Third, there arises the spectre of competition for resources. Each party involved is apprehensive of the other. Currently the universities are seen as trying either to suppress the polytechnics by stifling their development, or to absorb the polytechnics under the umbrella of the UGC, where, so the fable goes, they will be quietly throttled to death. On the other hand, universities concerned with a diminution of their influence in higher education attribute this to the malevolent activities of polytechnics. All of which is in fact nonsense, or near nonsense; no such plot and cabal exist.

To recapitulate: I do not think that in other than marginal matters and in matters of social contact there is yet much scope for transbinary cooperation. This is because:
1. The functions of universities and polytechnics differ.
2. The exchange of material goods and facilities cannot indefinitely continue in one direction only.
3. There needs to be much more mutual understanding.
In fact the dialogue is only just beginning. I have no doubt that it needs to continue and indeed be intensified to produce something worthwhile. I now turn to a discussion of the means for achieving this.

The first means of promoting mutual understanding between the universities and the polytechnics is to bring their finance to a common basis. Both universities and polytechnics claim that they are able to operate at lower cost than the other. The claims conflict because of the different items included in the cost and the quite different methods of operation. The research component of cost is not as great in the polytechnics as in universities; but on the other hand universities deal with a far more homogeneous set of students. This produces a great simplification in administrative and organizational matters, with consequent cost benefits. Universities have far greater capital assets, for example in the form of buildings and libraries, which are reflected in costs in maintenance and running expenses; for polytechnics much of the provision that exists has to be paid for out of revenue. But universities have far higher allowances, for example in terms of catering resources, than polytechnics. And so on; the list could be extended considerably.

The vast difference that exists in amenity between universities and polytechnics is undeniable, and has caused a great deal of concern on the part of both staff and students. In academic terms there is the assumption, previously noted, that better learning takes place in a 'better', that is to say more medieval, atmosphere. And it is undeniable that environment does affect mental set. Colour, form, warmth, absence of noise all go to influence how we feel and therefore how we think at a given time. But poor environment can be overriden by motivation. A good environment is wholly desirable; it may not in the extreme event be essential.

The wholly desirable equality of environment has caused one currently influential body to declare itself for an end to the binary system. The National Union of Students has advocated a 'polyversity' structure. The NUS feels that the only way to achieve substantial expansion lies in the massive restructuring of higher education. Institutions should be merged locally to form new, comprehensive centres of higher education. The polyversity would provide a range of courses as wide as that at present covered by the universities, the polytechnics and the colleges of education combined. Both full- and part-time education should be offered at varying levels to suit the individual student needs. One great advantage of polytechnics (that of the facility to switch from one level of course to another) should be retained and enlarged. The whole system would be coordinated nationally through a Higher Education Commission.

The NUS has attacked the binary system as 'educationally unsound', but has not given reasons for its putative unsoundness; the detailed comments on shortcomings of the binary system refer mainly to resources. Thus, the NUS is in favour of reciprocal arrangements between student unions; sharing of academic facilities for joint courses between polytechnics and universities; discussions between LEAs and universities for area accommodation bureaux, health centres and appointments boards. It calls for documentation on the wastage, both human and capital, that the binary system leads to – but wastage is seen very much through distortions produced by the myth of educational apartheid. This is a myth because, as I have tried to show, universities and polytechnics are doing different jobs. Yet one must appreciate that, for a student, the scene is immediate and confused; all he or she is able to ingest is that another student following a degree course elsewhere has better facilities, or worse ones. The NUS naturally wants its members treated equally, and regards this situation as intolerable. And so it is; but provision of equally distinguished amenities will not make the functions of polytechnics and universities the same.

The second means of increasing mutual understanding between the universities and polytechnics is for polytechnics to set up, on a collective basis, an effective parallel to the Committee of Vice-Chancellors and Principals (CVCP). This body is a successful consultative and liaison committee both between universities themselves and between universities and their varied external publics. A similar Committee of Polytechnic Directors has now been set up, and has similar functions to the CVCP. More important, these two organizations can now begin to talk to each other through a variety of formal and informal channels, set up joint working parties, and so on. These working parties would be able to consider the type of problem which so concerns the NUS; given the need to report back to a joint CVCP/Directors' Committee some progress might, in time, be made.

A third means of enhancing mutual understanding, which will probably follow from the joint committee, is greater representation from one type of institution to the other. At present, save in very few cases, representation is almost entirely in one direction: universities are represented on governing bodies of polytechnics, on committees of the CNAA, and so on. I cannot recall any case where there is direct polytechnic representation on the council or senate of a university (although one or two cases exist where polytechnic staff, in other capacities, serve on university bodies of various kinds). This one-way traffic is undesirable, mainly because it gives university staff an insight into inner workings of polytechnics, and does not give opportunity for information flow in the reverse direction. I have no doubt that reciprocity of representation *could* be arranged, and would be a great source of beneficial interaction.

A corollary of this view is that universities must allow their doors to be opened to research on them by polytechnics in exactly the same way as the polytechnics are opening their doors to investigation of their procedures by universities. A further corollary is that the role of polytechnics as an 'equally distinguished' partner in higher education needs to be recognized by the government in setting up various types of inquiries. It is probably no longer good enough to have royal commissions, say, in which academic expertise and educational representation are drawn wholly from universities. If the government of the day does not believe that polytechnics have any contribution to make in this sphere, it should say so.

As important as these ideas are, they do not sufficiently penetrate to the heart of the matter. The reality of transbinary cooperation, as distinct from its outer manifestation, is likely to occur when the means of allocation of finance is uniform for polytechnics and is comparable overall with the finance for universities. For this process to be started some body paralleling the UGC needs to be set up. It has tentatively been called the Polytechnic Grants Committee (PGC). It would function in a very similar way to the UGC, having its own secretariat, liaison with relevant ministries and government departments, etc. The output mechanism is easy enough to describe and I do it below (p. 153); the input mechanism, the source from which the PGC draws its funds, is much more a matter for political decision. The advent of the PGC would confront the local education authorities with the choice of either opting out altogether or – more likely – agreeing to contribute to the income of the PGC in return for a number of seats round the table. The latter would probably be more acceptable to the central government, which is assiduous in its efforts to retain local elements in the organization of higher education. If higher education in polytechnics were organized on the basis of the PGC, it is possible that one feature of the present system of financing public-sector higher education would come to an end. This is the use of a 'pool' to which all the LEAs contribute on the basis of a formula concerned with rateable value and population. Polytechnics draw, or rather recoup, their expenditure from this pool in proportion to the amount of work of various levels they do; the proportion for most polytechnics is tending towards 100 per cent. The system has become unpopular with LEAs since they have realized that it is open-ended and can only be controlled by individual vigilance.

The PGC would, however, be much more than a mere reorganization of the methods of allocating finance. Because finance must be concerned with the activities that an institution undertakes, the PGC would become involved with forward planning of polytechnics. This means that it would in effect become the coordinating body for polytechnics. From a financial vantage-point two appropriate major committees of the PGC could deal with approval of estimates, divided into two parts as follows:

1. That on which no policy decision is needed, i.e. relatively static expenditure for continuation of the service in substantially the same form as hitherto (due allowance being made for emergencies, replacements, etc.).

2. That on which major policy decisions are required, including major new equipment, substantial expansion of courses, staffing and so on.

The two major committees could deal with these parts of estimates both as a matter of speed and also as a matter of principle, since different criteria would be involved. Static expenditure could be dealt with annually, and developmental expenditure triennially. This means that polytechnics should put forward both three-year estimates and one-year estimates, the developmental estimates being on a rolling basis – approved three years in advance, but reviewed from year to year.

Clearly enough the PGC would become involved in two other main exercises. The first would be a study of cost effectiveness of polytechnics, investigating by use of, for example, operational-research techniques, matters such as optimum teaching times, distribution of space problems, and so on. If this were to lead to pressures for changes in the overall system of organization within each polytechnic, such changes should be made.

The second main exercise would be forward planning of polytechnic development in terms of numbers of students and types of courses. The PGC could start this exercise by asking each polytechnic to produce a coherent statement of its projected development over, say, the next four years in terms of the polytechnic as a whole, linked to and presumably preceded by a coherent statement of educational development ideas. Certainly the statement should include projections for growth or decline of demand for certain types of courses. Equally the statement should include details of cost per student-place in various categories. The PGC in reviewing these statements and facts should then produce a plan giving general levels and areas of work to be undertaken by each polytechnic, again on a rolling basis. Polytechnics should have the discretion to operate individual courses within this approved plan. There would be reasonable grounds for the PGC to encourage those polytechnics which had both educational ideas and which had demonstrated their ability to operate economically.

The PGC operating in this way would cause polytechnics to opt out of the present system of course approval, but there is nothing inconsistent in this. The regional advisory councils which advise on course approval have for some time been working under two difficulties: first, they can take no account of what universities do; and second, the recommendations of RACs are reviewed nationally. The PGC plan would automatically overcome the second difficulty. In respect of the universities, it would naturally lead into the form of liaison now to be described.

There is every reason for considering the development of higher education on a national basis; finance and development of courses are no exception to the rule. If a PGC is set up on the lines described above, it would easily be able to deal with the distribution of courses over the polytechnic field. It could go further and liaise with the UGC – which exerts various formal and informal controls over the distribution of work between universities – to ensure that in the first instance there was less duplication of provision. At a later stage growth areas could be discussed and agreements made on how matters were to be handled. As with the CVCP and the Committee of Polytechnic Directors, more could probably be achieved by a number of working parties operating within an agreed framework than by a formal union of the two bodies concerned. Any thought of having a Higher Education Commission (for other than nominal functions) would in political terms be a non-starter. The Higher Education Commission, if it were executive, would in effect be another branch of the Department of Education and Science. I see no need for this.

The natural question that arises at this stage is: Why have two bodies, that is, two committees of top men in the institutions, two committees for forward planning and finance (UGC and

PGC)? The answer in the simplest terms is that *the two social organizations, the polytechnics and the universities, are doing different jobs*. To try to force them into the same administrative mould using the same criteria for making decisions would cause irreparable damage to one party or the other.

As a final example, consider that the citizens in the Manchester area have on three previous occasions built up an educational organization to do locally the job that the polytechnics are undertaking for society as a whole. If Manchester Polytechnic becomes absorbed in the UGC they will have to do it yet again. I am not sure that even Manchester can afford it.

Charles Carter

A Comprehensive System

In contrast to the views just expressed, many people see serious disadvantages in continuing the separate development of two sectors, however substantial the cooperation between them. University opinion, in particular, has been disturbed by the assumption sometimes made that the local authority part of the binary system should carry the main burdens of expansion. The provocative words of successive ministers on the place of the public-sector colleges should perhaps be allowed to pass into kindly oblivion; the belief that this is the only way to get higher education on the cheap does not seem likely to survive contact with the facts. A more serious objection to polytechnic expansion is the likelihood of a mismatch between course provision, and student desires and qualifications. This is because the local-authority sector in the binary system (other than the colleges of education) has grown out of technical colleges and colleges of commerce and art. The first and most natural activity for such institutions is to duplicate technological and scientific courses which are already available, in excess of demand, in the universities: so that, for instance, there might be two half-empty courses in metallurgy in the same town, one in a university and one in a polytechnic. The second natural activity is to extend work in the social sciences and in management subjects. Courses in this area will be available to many students (for the entrance qualifications need not be as specific as in technology and science), and some increase in provision is certainly needed. There are some who doubt, however, whether the training of numerous sociologists and economists is really a productive exercise, and questions are already being asked about the proliferation of courses in the management subjects. It is much less natural for polytechnics and similar institutions (headed, as they so often are, by scientists and engineers) to produce imaginative ideas for the general education of arts-based students. But this is where talent is in most danger of being denied opportunities of higher education.

There is a limit to the extent to which it is possible (let alone sensible) to push people into vocational courses in which they have no strong interest by denying them the opportunity of doing anything else. The universities have thus seen the polytechnics and the other colleges as operating in the most over-supplied parts of the higher-education market; and the depressed status, in some colleges, of 'liberal studies' as an ancillary subject (in comparison with the prestige of corresponding studies in universities) does not encourage a belief that the colleges could readily move to supply the shortage areas.

These are the doubts of interested parties and, though they receive some confirmation from what is so far known about new developments in the public sector, it would be a powerful answer if the polytechnics replied that they propose to use their own new freedoms of government to create new types of course, appropriate to student desires and qualifications. But a yet more serious doubt would remain. Into the discussion of the binary system there has now crept the dismal phrase 'parity of esteem'. The universities and the public-sector colleges are to be equal but different, helpfully differentiated but enjoying the same status. We have been here before: secondary-modern schools and grammar schools were to enjoy 'parity of esteem', but they never obtained it, and the reorganization into comprehensive schools (which, despite all the fuss at the margins, is widely supported in the country and in both political parties) became necessary to put right a gross psychological error.

The school problem was dramatized by the eleven-plus examination. Though designed to offer children and their parents helpful guidance about the most appropriate school, this examination was almost universally regarded as one which was 'passed' to go to a grammar school and 'failed' to go to a secondary modern school. It takes but little acquaintance with sixth forms to see a similar process in operation. Those likely to do well in 'A' level examinations mostly regard themselves as a university stream. Those very unlikely to get to a university are encouraged to apply to a college of education or to a public-sector college; they swell the numbers of those who give such a college as first preference (see p. 27), but this is because they have a constrained choice. Of course it is possible to find brilliant students who have chosen not to go to a university, just as it is possible to find active Conservative trade unionists. The public-sector colleges receive an entry from some who left school early because of poor academic progress, and then, developing late, pass by the ONC path to higher education. Nevertheless the broad picture is one in which there is plainly *not* parity of esteem, and in which a considerable number of those who go to higher education outside the universities regard themselves as having 'failed'.

My university has a research project on such people, and on the related group of those who just manage to get a university place. The results so far available suggest that the 'seventeen-plus' creates a problem very similar to that observed earlier with the 'eleven-plus', namely that those who 'fail' set themselves for the future lower norms of effort than those who 'succeed'. It is as though they have been classed as belonging to the dimmer part of the population, and intend for the future to live up to their reputation. This attitude will seem to many people unreasonable and unnecessary, just as it seemed to enlightened men that children who narrowly failed to get into a grammar school ought to have been happier and more successful in a secondary modern school. But it often did not work that way. Failure to take account of the effect of a divisive examination leads to a loss of talents which ought to be developed.

I do not feel any confidence that parity of esteem can be established in a divided system of higher education. The problem is perhaps a little easier, because industrialists (especially from the smaller firms) genuinely do esteem the products of strongly vocational CNAA degree courses. But this esteem is sometimes for the wrong reasons – a preference for those who fit neatly into an existing pattern of skill requirements, rather than those educated to be adaptable to new needs twenty years ahead; in any case it is neither universal, nor strong enough to be decisive in influencing student choice. It is clear from what I have written (especially on pp. 81–5) that I want to see a highly varied and differentiated system of higher education; but I also want each part of this system to attract its appropriate talent, and to have no sense of being a second or lower choice. I see no way of achieving this but to make higher education comprehensive.

A comprehensive system of higher education could not be like

a series of comprehensive schools. The elements to be included –
courses of differing length and level, a range of subjects, vocational and non-vocational interests, full-time and part-time study,
research and other activities related to teaching – are too extensive
to be successsfully developed in one institution, unless it were
to be of a size so great as to cause serious problems of management and of lack of contact with individual students. Therefore
we must imagine some kind of federation of institutions, with
distances between them which in some instances would be substantial. Would such a federation have any real value, or would
it resemble the efforts of some local authorities to create a comprehensive school by employing a signwriter to put the same
name outside several separated premises? The conditions of
success would be: first, that the students should be effectively
members of a single community; second, that the staff should
have a common professional loyalty; and third, that there should
be some broad policy of the federation within which the separate
units would develop – like the policy of a large company, such
as ICI, in relation to its separate divisions.

The unity of the student body would not be difficult to achieve.
Students are already impatient of class-divisions between different institutions; they would welcome a common access to
student facilities, joint housing schemes, and so on. The sense
of unity among staff would be much more difficult to create.
There would, I am sure, be much goodwill, among the younger
and less stuffy university staff, and among the staff of the polytechnics and colleges, for the idea of a single professional group-
ing – especially if this implied a more even access to libraries and
research facilities. But there are different salary structures, and
different 'trade unions', involved; the problems which appeared
when the colleges of advanced technology were assimilated to
the university system would be multiplied.

Undoubtedly, however, the chief obstacle would be the change
in control needed to achieve a general policy within each cluster
or federation of institutions. We can perhaps leave on one side
the special difficulty of the pockets of higher-level work which
will continue to exist in further-education institutions other
than polytechnics. Unless the federation covered all *further*
education (which would be a great additional complication) the

best solution would probably be to link this higher-level work rather as work in the colleges of education is now linked to the universities: that is, to place on the federation the task of approving the qualication offered and the arrangements made for teaching, without transferring the ownership of buildings or the employment of staff. The central group of a federation might then consist of a university, a polytechnic, some colleges of education, and perhaps in future some junior colleges. I do not believe that the necessary coordination of policy between these could be achieved if they remained in divided ownership. This is not a matter of lack of goodwill; experience of trying to achieve common action between systems with an entirely different administrative structure suggests that far too much energy runs to waste in trying to get the systems to work simultaneously and with harmony.

It would therefore be logically necessary either to transfer universities to local-authority control, or to transfer the local-authority colleges to universities (as, in relation to colleges of education, Robbins recommended), or to devise a new type of organization to cover both. I do not consider that local goverment in this country is, or will become after reorganization, strong enough to be the sole instrument for running higher education; in any case (as will be seen from pp. 111–13) I consider that there is much virtue in a genuine autonomy of higher-education institutions. On the other hand, I do not think that the present constitution of universities is appropriate to the control of a federation of colleges. It would generally be operated so as to make the university itself a sort of holding company, with final authority over the actions of its subsidiaries. The relations needed in a comprehensive system are not those of master and servant.

I see no alternative, therefore, to progressive action under the royal prerogative to set aside the charters of universities, and substitute new charters appropriate to the government of a cluster of cooperating institutions. These charters would have to provide for a broadly representative council for the cluster, and for a set of academic bodies, not constructed as a hierarchy, for the constituent colleges. If this were done, it would be appropriate that each federation or cluster (there might be some forty or fifty in Great Britain) should receive grant-aid from a central Higher Education Grants Committee, constituted on much the same principle, and with much the same traditions, as the University Grants Committee. But I see no point in creating such a committee *without* bringing the institutions together at the local level; there would be limited value in a body which had the job of financing two entirely separate systems.

It must by now be clear that, even if the case for a comprehensive system for higher education is accepted as strong, it would be an act of great political courage to create such a system, for it would involve standing up to the local authorities in a way which no recent government has ventured. Nevertheless, it is desirable that the implications of a comprehensive system should be investigated boldly and thoroughly: the difficulties may seem less if they are fully known.

Peter Venables
A Comment

The question is not one of great political courage, but of political feasibility and educational desirability. Shotgun marriages of unequal institutions will provide no harmonious lasting partnerships. There are some basic facts of life in higher education which should not be glossed over. First of all, the institutions of higher education are unequal in size, endowments, amenities, range of subjects, scope of research, and the distinction of staff and intellectual attainments. They differ also in the effectiveness of their relationships with and service to the community at large, and to industry and the professions in particular. This is true within each sector of the binary system, and the range is even larger across the great divide. The brief descriptions of universities in chapter 2 omits the most important aspect of all – the comparative range of attainments and scholarship, of discovery and application, the standards of excellence of particular universities, and of many departments within a much larger number of universities. The new universities and the former colleges of advanced technology know at first hand the exacting standards of the long-established universities, and in their short lives have striven to attain comparable standards, and in some instances have in fact reached notable standards of excellence. Through their links with the universities the colleges of education have made varying progress in academic and professional standards, and some excel. The technical colleges and other further-education institutions have likewise made varying progress, and those now reorganized as polytechnics have made progress under the influence over a long period of the London external degree system; in recent years they have been influenced by the supervision of the CNAA for the recognition of degree courses. But, compared with the universities, the colleges of education and the polytechnics respectively differ far more widely in the basic facts of academic life listed above. For example, polytechnics range from one which has twenty-one courses recognized by the CNAA, down to five which each have five or less. This reflects the present position, not the potential; nevertheless the fact is that they are by no means a homogeneous group.

In the second place there is a practicable limit to the disparity and diversity containable within any system, or any institution whether federated or not. Contrariwise conforming influences are ever present which tend to reduce diversity, and may indeed distort the basic orientation and purpose of the institution (p. 97). To offset these influences, the first requirement is to facilitate the emergence of institutions by a system of accreditation to the point of enabling them to become chartered institutions in their own right and of their own kind (p. 139). They might remain single institutions, or become part of a federated institution still protected as chartered institutions – as Imperial College within London University, and Manchester Institute of Science and Technology within Manchester University – or on a more dispersed scale, the constituent parts of the federated University of Wales. Such relationships should be fostered on a reasonable scale within the particular regions, and not inhibited as at present; but they should not be mandatory.

Changes in the system of national administration should be consonant with such regional changes, and should help them to achieve a rapid evolution. A Higher Education Grants Committee for the polytechnics and colleges of education in parallel with the University Grants Committee, with significant cross-membership and similarly related to the DES, would be the best way to operate for three quinquennial periods. Valuable experience would thus be gained in planning and development, in the clarification of functions, the interrelatedness of institutions, as well as in the raising of standards and the chartering of institutions. A time-limit should be set to ensure that the objective of bringing all under one central committee will be constantly borne in mind – and achieved with decisive finality.

It will not do arbitrarily to abolish university charters – egalitarian action by downgrading can hardly achieve higher standards of excellence. Nor can a uniform pattern of regional federations overall be achieved – the proposals are eloquently silent on such difficult instances as, for example, Oxford, Cambridge and London. Such major exceptions to a general policy combined, for example, with SRC policy on concentration of research grants, could in a very short time drain away post-graduate work from other universities so as to make them sub-stantially undergraduate institutions, to the serious detriment of their teaching. Of course there are many problems to be solved, many patterns to be established, but Churchill remarked that 'it is an inconvenient rule that nothing can be done until every-thing can be done'. We need progressive action over a clearly defined time-scale, rather than premature plastic surgery.

Chapter Eight
Meeting the Cost Restraint

At this point Richard Layard and Gareth Williams bring the
discussion back to the hard problem of money. However
organized, the expansion must be expensive. If the national
economy continues to stagnate the cost may seem insupportably
high, involving unreasonable diversions of resources from other
important social aims. If a high growth rate in the economy is
achieved the problem will seem much easier, but will certainly not
be trivial. It is therefore important to look at some of the means
of saving resources without risk to quality: exploitation of
economies of scale, increased teaching hours, better use of
advanced educational technology, savings in building costs,
student loans and so on. The chapter reaches the encouraging
conclusion that, with the adoption of the significant forms of
cost-saving, there need be no cost constraint preventing an
expansion on the scale suggested by chapter 2. But Peter
Venables, in an addendum, draws attention to some of the
disadvantages and problems of the types of cost-saving suggested.
There is, in fact, no way of dodging the need to weigh costs
against benefits, and the financial results of methods of
cost-saving against their educational disadvantages, even though
many of the items in the balance are difficult or impossible to
quantify. In other words, there must in the end be an act of
political judgement.

Richard Layard and
Gareth Williams

The cost of all the developments we have considered will be tremendous. If inputs per student remain constant, the proportion of the GNP absorbed in the direct costs of full-time higher education will rise from 0·9 per cent in 1966–7 to 1·8 per cent in 1981–2. And maintenance grants at present rates would rise from nearly 0·3 per cent to nearly 0·5 per cent of the GNP (see Table 6, p. 39).

So what? it is sometimes said. One should decide what to spend by comparing benefits and costs, and not looking at costs alone. This is quite true, but there are two good reasons for looking at the costs of higher education very closely. The first is that the direct costs of higher education are carried almost wholly by public funds, and so by definition are maintenance grants. Both Labour and Conservative parties are now committed to holding constant (or reducing) the share of public expenditure in the GNP. Though one may disagree with these policies, there is clearly going to be severe financial pressure in education. Such pressure was of course forecast for the 1960s, but a crisis was averted partly because the public sector's share of the GNP rose somewhat and partly because of remarkable cuts in the share of the GNP going to defence. Both these happy changes are now over. A rise in education's *share* will henceforth require a *fall* for health, social security, roads or police. Yet on present policies education's share will rise from about 5·5 per cent of the GNP in 1966 to 8 per cent in 1980.[1] Something will surely have to give. It could be primary education or secondary, or the further education of those who leave school at sixteen. But it does seem fair that higher education should bear its bit. One solution of course is to shift some of the financial burden from taxpayers on to

1. For two independent, and very different, estimates arriving at this same result see *Planning for Education in 1980*, Fabian Research Series, no. 282, 1970, and K. Ollerenshaw, 'Predictions of education expenditure', *Local Government Finance*, May 1970.

students. The case for this is strong, and we shall argue later for some reduction in the public subsidy of students' maintenance. But the direct costs are likely to go on being met by the taxpayer, and here too it is only fair that some savings should be made.

A second argument for this is independent of the constraints of public finance. It is simply that wherever it is possible to achieve the same result more cheaply, the cheaper method should be preferred; and there do seem to be long-run possibilities of cost-saving in higher education. At the famous meeting in late 1969 between Shirley Williams (then Minister of State for Higher Education), the UGC and the CVCP no less than thirteen suggestions were made. These have since been commented on by the Vice-Chancellors Committee [1] and we shall confine ourselves to only a few of them. The argument will be illustrated mainly with reference to the universities, but applies equally to all sectors.

Saving on teacher costs: economies of scale

There are two ways to cut expenditure – by cutting costs per student (real costs, costs to public funds, or both) and by reducing the number of students. We are only interested in the first. The most obvious method here is to let the staff–student ratio decline. Labour costs form a high proportion of the direct costs of higher education, and each year labour grows more and more expensive in terms of goods. (It is not, however, the case that higher education is more labour-intensive than the economy as a whole.) There are two ways in which labour can be saved in higher education, neither of which would of course involve redundancy, but merely a less than proportional growth in the teaching force.

The first way is by exploiting the available economies of scale. If one compares the pattern of teaching in large and small departments one sees that the large ones can, with a given staff–student ratio, provide students with a given pattern of teaching at the cost of shorter teaching hours by the staff. The point is

1. For the original suggestions see Committee of Vice-Chancellors and Principals, *University Development in the 1970s*, and for the Committee's comments, *University Development in the 1970s: A Statement of Views by the Committee*, April 1970.

illustrated in Table 13, which shows the average pattern of teaching in all universities in 1961. For each type of teaching (as shown in each row) the average hours which teachers spend on it must necessarily equal the average hours which students

Table 13
Teaching Arrangements in Universities (averages in Spring Term 1962)

	Hours a week given per teacher	*Hours a week received per student*	*Student– staff ratio*	*Class size*
Lectures	2·5	7·1	8·0	23·0
Discussion periods	3·5	1·5	8·0	3·6
Practicals	3·2	3·4	8·0	8·4
Written exercise classes	0·5	0·4	8·0	7·3
Totals	9·7*	12·4	*Averages* 8·0	10·4

Source : Robbins, Appendix Two (B), p. 351.

*The figure 9·7 in column 1 includes an allowance for teaching given by postgraduate students.

spend receiving it, multiplied by the student–staff ratio divided by the size of class. It follows that if the size of classes can be doubled, the average teaching hours of the staff can be halved. For some types of teaching – discussion groups, for example – the whole quality of the event depends on the size of class, and the same result cannot possibly be got if the size of class is doubled. On the other hand, for lectures the amount of benefit per student may fall little as the size of audience grows. And a doubling of lecture audiences would cut average teaching by over one hour a week – let alone its effect on preparation time.

By the same token, if staff teaching hours were to be held constant and student hours likewise, an increase in class sizes would clearly permit an increase in the student–staff ratio. Since the average size of universities will nearly double over the period, the economies which can be reaped on this score are considerable.

But scale has the further advantage of permitting greater specialization, which not only raises quality but means that individual teachers can teach a narrower and more closely related group of subjects. So one might expect that they could teach longer hours for a given total time spent on teaching and preparation for teaching. Would it really be unreasonable for staff to teach a little more than they do? In 1962 academic staff spent on average eight hours a week on face-to-face teaching. A good part of the rest of their 40-hour week was devoted directly to other activities on students' behalf (see Table 14), and there

Table 14
Average Working Hours per Week of University Teachers (in Spring Term 1962)

Teaching	8
Preparation	4
Correction	2
Research	11
Private study	5
Administration	5
Other university work	4
Non-university work	2
Total	41

Source : Robbins, Appendix Three, p. 56 (freely rounded).

may in any case have been some increase in total and in teaching hours since 1962. Nevertheless some modest increase still seems possible, and we should surely be able to accommodate a fall in the staff–student ratio of say 20 per cent – from 1:8 to 1:9·6. On average this would require one and a half hours extra face-to-face teaching a week from each teacher. Yet the cost consequences are enormous. Suppose it only affected the academic salary bill, reducing it by 17 per cent; current tuition cost in universities would fall by 8·5 per cent, or £50 million in 1981–2. But the effects might well be wider. Secretaries and technicians and even administrators may, to a large extent, be complementary to rather than substitutes for academic staff. If all salaries fell by 17 per cent, we should save £75 million in 1981–2. If the government is looking for areas of flexibility in the system, where change is politically possible, it surely lies here more than anywhere else, and the vice-chancellors have, to their credit, endorsed the idea of some change of unspecified magnitude in staff–student ratios.

Saving on teacher costs: educational technology

Yet even with such a change the costs are still very high. This leads us to the second standard method of saving labour – by the substitution of capital for it. In higher education the ratio of capital to labour is still largely adjusted to their relative prices in the Middle Ages. If proper attention were paid to the cost of students' time and teachers' time relative to the price of books, most universities would have far more books and articles readily available to students, and fewer teachers. The annual services of a university teacher cost as much as the annual services of about five thousand books. At existing staff–book ratios, the books seem a better bargain for many institutions. Moreover students often waste hours looking for books. If a student spends two hours a week doing this and he could be earning £700 a year, the annual time wasted is worth £35 per student or £35,000 per 1,000 students, a sum which would buy quite a few books.

But, though the technical progress of the fifteenth century has not yet been fully assimilated, a new wave of technical progress is now upon us, which gives promise of far more striking economies. This is the revolution that began with films and has gone on through audio-tape to video-tape, whereby people will soon be able to borrow a lecture from the library and play it at their own speed on their own television set. The revolution has already of course transformed the industries of communication and entertainment, of which one would have supposed education to be a part. Instead we are still often told that education has special problems of teacher–student relationships, which make it totally unsuited to technical innovation. The anxieties here are genuine, and it is important for people to realize that the new media could humanize rather than dehumanize the educational process. At present a great part of teaching consists of basic exposition, rather than of interchange and discussion between staff and students. Such basic exposition is difficult and requires a good deal of preparation by the teacher. Even then it is often indifferently done, either for lack of time or talent, since all teachers are not equally good at it. We thus have a system where, for example, about a hundred lecture courses in first-year economics are being given in the country as a whole, each in complete isolation yet using fundamentally similar syllabuses. We exploit neither the economies of scale that go with the pooling of resources nor the special talents of particular teachers. Whereas our present hundred lecture courses may cost about £50,000 a year,[1] we could certainly for less cost present three or four competing courses of recorded lectures. And some of the cost saved could be devoted to running more elaborate systems of classes, where problems were discussed using, if the teachers wished, problems and worksheets prepared by the specialist lecturers.

One very proper objection to this idea is that each university wants to run a slightly different course from every other one. However, this only means that packages should consist of modules of sub-courses which can be used in different combinations for different purposes. The fact that courses vary does not prevent teachers recommending textbooks written by others, and the same should be true of other forms of packaged exposition. Another objection is that this approach will divide teachers into stars and helots. But it need not. At present in large departments most people both give lectures and take classes associated with lectures given by others. We only want to see this principle extended to the national level.

This is already happening to a small extent. Six northern universities have combined to produce a computer course in which no exposition is needed by a live instructor, though there is of course plenty of live interchange between staff and students. But the Open University is the real test, and much will depend on its impact on the rest of the higher-education system, which could be far more important than its contribution to its own students. Apart from this, neither the government nor the UGC has paid adequate attention to the new educational technology. The UGC has established centres for one or other of the tech-

---

1. Assuming that university teachers are paid on average £2,500 a year, and give two hours of lectures a week on average. The calculation assumes that these lectures (with their related tutorial and other work) represent 40 per cent of the work they are paid for by the university.

nologies in eight universities. But most of the work done so far seems to have been peripheral to the basic teaching task of the universities – on aids rather than substitutes for it.

What accounts for the slow rate of progress? In the main, teachers have not come forward with proposals for the packaging of major courses. The work involved is very considerable, and people are not prepared to do it unless they can expect a reasonably wide distribution of the product – it would in any case be uneconomic otherwise. This seems to require that projects of this kind be sponsored by some national body – something like a Schools Council for higher education. The UGC's subject committees, and professional bodies such as the Royal Society, the Royal Economic Society and the like, seem obvious existing sponsors. Some progress has been made in promoting projects on generally acceptable lines on statistics for biologists, and accountancy and other subjects for engineers. It is natural that progress should be easiest in the area of service teaching, which is the least popular among academics. But ultimately it will have to affect the basic bread-and-butter teaching where the big costs lie. If the universities do not act now they will be forced to when money becomes tighter. In further education, where there are national syllabuses and national examinations at craftsman level and very similar syllabuses throughout the country for National Certificate courses, the scope for educational technology is even greater, yet very little seems to be happening. If further education wishes to prove its capacity for innovation it needs to get moving. But whatever packages are produced, it would of course be entirely up to the individual institution whether it used them – exactly as with textbooks today.

The new technology will of course cost money. Non-teaching inputs per student will rise : they have been doing so anyway. (In this sense our cost projections in chapter 2 may be conservative – non-teaching inputs per student in universities rose for example between 1961–2 and 1964–5 by no less than 18 per cent, whereas we assume they will remain constant in future.) But the saving of staff could be much more than any of the figures quoted earlier. Unless technical progress of this kind occurs in higher education we shall continue in the grip of Baumol's disease, whereby an unprogressive industry whose output grows in step with the national product absorbs an ever-growing proportion of the nation's man-power.[1]

Saving on building costs

Apart from labour the biggest cost item in higher education is buildings. The main cost-saving proposal here is to extend the academic year. This aims mainly to spread the fixed cost of capital over more students, thus reducing the cost per student. But, as chapter 2 showed, the capital cost per student is only 18 per cent of the total direct cost – a good deal less than is popularly imagined. An increase in the academic year from thirty to forty-five weeks would thus appear to reduce the direct cost per student by only 6 per cent. The savings might of course be more than this, for though the proposal does not envisage that teachers teach more over the year, it might well have the effect of permitting more economic use of secretaries, porters and technicians, some of whom are in disguised unemployment for part of the vacations. Even so the savings are unlikely to approach those to be had from 20 per cent longer teaching hours in term, and one would suppose most teachers would prefer the latter.

Leaving this aside, there may still be scope for reductions in unit capital costs. For academic accommodation it is encouraging that the CVCP believe that a major expansion could be 'associated with a rate of capital expenditure per student significantly lower than that over the Robbins years'. For residential accommodation there have already been reductions in real unit cost, and these costs are in any case now being shifted increasingly on to students, owing to the UGC's unwillingness to finance further residential building. The social cost of residence might be further reduced by steps to encourage students to live at home. If maintenance grants were the same irrespective of where you studied, some more students might live at home; though it seems more likely that, in the high-wage economy towards which we are moving, most students who wanted to would find the money to get away from home.

1. See W. Baumol, 'Macroeconomics of unbalanced growth', *American Economic Review*, June 1967.

Student loans

Unlike the earlier proposals, student loans would not affect the social cost per student, but merely its incidence. The aim is not to reduce the resource cost of education but its cost to the taxpayer. The case for loans is based on equity. Most students, being abler or from more privileged homes than the average taxpayer, would, even if they did not go to college, end up richer than average. So why should they in addition be provided by the taxpayer with a present (subsidy) equal to three years' wages of the average working man? The effect of this subsidized education is to make their subsequent income still higher. This is redistribution from the poor to the rich, if we think of people in terms of their lifetime incomes.

It is of course true that not all of the benefits of educating a student accrue to the student himself rather than to other members of society, and this constitutes a good ground for some subsidy. It is also true that, if a man's education raises his income, it also raises the taxes he pays. However, the discounted value of these extra taxes is at present very small compared with the subsidy, and there does seem a case for reducing the subsidy somewhat.

Against this it is sometimes argued that students are after all working at college, so why should they not be paid for doing so? Now it is quite true that students are working in a capital goods industry, building human capital. As such they could either be paid for their work, in which case like other workers in those industries they would have no title to the returns on the capital they have created; or they could work for nothing and own the capital. The loan proposal amounts to saying that to the extent that their maintenance, as students, is paid by the State, graduates should surrender to the State a corresponding share in the returns to that education.

A particular merit of the proposal from the student's point of view is that, if open-ended, it allows him to decide how much he wants to be supported now, at the expense of gaining lesser returns in future. Thus students can choose their own standard of living, balancing their present against their future needs. This is particularly important for older students, and without something like this it is hard to see how the massive re-training effort, which is universally advocated, will ever actually happen.

There are, however, a number of problems with loan schemes which need to be faced. The most serious is the danger that people, especially from working-class backgrounds, will be afraid to incur debt, when the returns from which to repay it are so uncertain. The education of an individual is certainly much more risky than many forms of business investment, which is one of the reasons why the State supports education, being able to pool the risks. However, this problem can be easily got round by making the amount of repayment depend on subsequent income – for each £100 borrowed you repay x per cent of your subsequent income, collection being made via income tax (probably subject to a maximum repayment). Some economists object to this on grounds of efficiency, but that argument overlooks the strong efficiency case for the pooling of risks, where this is possible. The method proposed has also the political advantage that it protects the lower-paid professions and non-earning women.

But what about the problem of students from working-class homes? They certainly perceive the returns from higher education less clearly than middle-class students and may have a higher aversion to risk. They therefore need differential inducements to stay on. A loan scheme would not rule this out. There could be differential terms of borrowing (smaller x); or, more simply, a differential grant element could remain in parallel with a system of loans.

The key point of course is at what level the public subsidy to students should be set. Some writers have argued that students should pay full cost fees, mostly privately financed from loans, as well as providing their own maintenance. A change of this magnitude is politically inconceivable, and we are only concerned here with raising students' contributions to maintenance. When one considers how a loan scheme might be introduced at undergraduate level, one possibility would be to freeze grants at their present money rates, and to give any increase in the form of loans. Inflation will then erode the real value of a given money grant; and inflation and real income growth will reduce the average money grant per student, as parental money incomes rise. This device has the merit of gradualism and also automatically preserves the differential advantages of poorer students.

People sometimes argue that switching to loans gives little help to the Exchequer, because the repayments come in so much later. In fact the saving could be considerable. Suppose that from 1971 £100 per year per student were provided for three years in the form of loans, and that the pattern of income-related repayments was designed to bring in on average the same flow as would the repayment of the same sum in fixed annual instalments over twenty years at a 5 per cent interest rate. Then the average repayment per person would be £24 a year for twenty years, and the total flow of repayments to the Exchequer would have built up to £32 million by 1981–2. Even with no further expansion in student numbers after then, repayments would mount to £90 million in 1991–2, and £118 million by 2001–2. These purely illustrative figures indicate substantial savings, if such aid were to replace outright grants which would otherwise have been made. (We assume that the amount of net-borrowing by the public sector is the same under both schemes. It would in principle be possible to finance the whole loan scheme by public-sector borrowing and to use the repayments to retire public dept; but we ignore this possibility.)

There remains the question of whether an effective reduction in student aid would affect the demand for higher education as well as the incidence of its cost. In theory it would be bound to do so, if the demand for education is at all price-elastic. In fact no one knows what the effect would be, which is an argument for proceeding gradually along the lines we have suggested. On balance the effect seems unlikely to be severe. In Scandinavia, where repayment is not related to subsequent income, no serious effects have been noted; the schemes seem to work smoothly.[1]

Other ideas

This brings us, finally, to the obvious point that one way to cut costs is to devise strategies for cutting the number of students. We would not support any policy that had that as its aim. But there are some important suggestions in the air, which have been

1. See M. A. Woodhall, *Student Loans: A Review of Experience in Scandinavia and Elsewhere*, Harrap, 1970.

advocated on these grounds but seem worth considering for other reasons.

The first is the proposal that students should be required to have worked for a year before coming up to college or university. The case for this is two-fold. First, some working experience helps to bring out the relevance and concrete significance of almost any line of study. But second, more students, when they go to college, should have a clearer idea of the jobs they ultimately wish to do. Only thus can we escape from the present situation where so many graduates end up in jobs where they cannot use their own specialist knowledge and wish they had studied something else. Compulsory employment before college may be going too far, but surely universities should encourage students to do a year's relevant work before coming up, and make it easy for them to do so. Perhaps the appointments boards could be made responsible for offering a placement service of this kind to all students accepted for entry to their university. The government might also consider offering slightly less favourable maintenance aid to students going straight on from school. Equally, if 'A' level were taken in December, for which there are other powerful arguments, many more students would have done a job. These are but a sample of ways in which this highly desirable development could be encouraged.

The other proposal we have in mind is for a two-year first degree, followed by a two-year Master's course for the more serious students. This proposal could either mean a four-year course for most with some leaving after two years, or the reverse. As formulated by Professor Pippard in discussions at Cambridge, it would be four years for 30 per cent and two for 70 per cent. This degree of selection would cause great bitterness, and if the selection were much less severe there would be no saving in costs. More sensible seems the idea of two plus one, rather than two plus two. That is, the universities and colleges should recognize that there are many students (say a quarter) who would gladly leave after two years, if they could take a qualification (say a diploma) with them, especially if they knew that they could get a degree by coming back later with some work experience for an extra year's study. Three years is a long time and there seems no sense in forcing people at eighteen to opt for three further years or nothing: at sixteen the option is a two-year course and at twenty-one there are one- and two-year Master's courses, so why three years from eighteen? If colleges could devise coherent courses which lasted two years with an optional third year, this would merely add a very desirable element of flexibility to the system. But it would be important not to pre-select at the beginning of the course those who would have two years only.

None of this would save much by way of costs. For that there is no alternative to a lower staff–student ratio, with more use of educational technology, some economies in capital expenditure, and some student loans. If these measures are adopted, there need be no cost constraint preventing an expansion on the scale we have suggested.

Peter Venables
A Comment

In chapter 4 it is assumed, in whatever changes may come, that economy and efficiency will be reasonably maintained throughout the system. On these grounds the arguments and considerations put forward in this present chapter concerning staff–student ratios, the use of books and audio-visual aids, the wider potential benefits of the Open University, and the use of buildings, are generally acceptable. Some proposals are, however, in a very different category because of the adverse effects they will have upon educational opportunities for students. For instance, though the proposal that a year should be inserted between school and university is often discussed, I do not know any good reason for believing that it is, or is generally thought, a good idea; though I am aware that, in aggressive reaction to student unrest, some assert that 'a touch of real life will sort them out'. Richard Layard and Gareth Williams deal with 'the obvious point that one way to cut costs is to devise strategies for cutting the number of students', and I am sure they speak for all the authors (and hopefully for a large number of readers) when they say 'we would not support any policy that had that as its *aim*' (italics mine) – nevertheless some proposals may have that *effect*. Presumably the aim of the intercalated year is educational, relying on the traumatic psycho-dynamic forces of the marketplace and the everyday world to promote in intelligent young men and women all those desirable changes of character and will, purpose and sensibility which the universities supposedly fail to achieve. If the educational problems of the Era of Consent are novel and difficult within the universities, they are unlikely to be solved by transferring them arbitrarily elsewhere into a predominantly non-educational environment. Will this period of 'beneficial employment' (educational history should give us pause) be equally applicable to all would-be full-time students in all tertiary institutions – polytechnics, colleges of education and so on – and if not why not?

The second idea put forward, of introducing student loans, is a far more difficult proposition to consider, as the case is stated to be based on equity. Again one has the uneasy feeling that *aim* and *effect* would turn out to be very different from each other, that specific economic objectives would entail widely differing adverse social effects, and perhaps adverse economic ones also. Moreover, non-quantifiable social benefits and amenities are notoriously difficult to justify on purely economic grounds. The history of economic progress is littered with the untoward effects of its by-products, as permanent in their way as the hitherto seemingly indestructible plastic litter accumulating around our shores, or the worse aspects of pollution (which will take a great deal of non-economic research to rectify).

The economic bases need further exploration and appraisal in the light of desirable social as well as economic objectives. The whole matter is very complex, and this comment permits only certain aspects and issues to be noted for further consideration.

What is the probable total tax to be repaid over the twenty-year period? What is the likely impact of this additional tax on differing professional and social groups? Will this loan system be applied only to full-time degree students? What about diploma students, and students in courses for professional qualifications? What about students in part-time courses, and what will be the repercussions on sponsorship of students by industry? The Industrial Training Board Levy encourages the larger firms to train more than they need as a general benefit to industry, without recoupment from the individual; will this prove to be an especially invidious case of economic paternalism, alongside a loans system? How long indeed would the present system persist unchanged? And how long would it resist the 'bonding' of students for several years after qualifying, with the untoward consequences for firms and employees experienced in other parts of the world? In recent years the armed forces have established attractive scholarship schemes for would-be graduates – would they be exempt from a loans scheme?

What is the probable effect on recruitment to different professions, according to the number of years required, three-year degree courses generally, four years for a professionally qualified graduate teacher, five or six years for medicine? What of those professions for which an M.Sc., and preferably a Ph.D., is increasingly required? Will grants now made by the research councils, SRC, SSRC and so on in future also become loans? If so, with what effect on recruitment? If not, why not? Could the reason be the need to secure wider social and economic benefits than the individual's own advancement? What about the increasing importance properly being attached to refresher, updating courses – 'recurrent re-investment in higher education' – are they to be primarily or wholly at the students' expense? The net effect would be to shift the onus of advancing knowledge and regenerating the theoretical basis and the practice of the professions from the State to the individual; and he (less frequently she) would in effect be asked to take on these wider responsibilities by investing their own future earnings (unknown and unpredictable) against all the unknown hazards of combined political and economic change (all this, mergers and the Common Market too). That this would be especially attractive to the older student, married and with increasing commitments, seems highly improbable: that it should be argued as the only likely basis of 'the massive retraining effort, which is universally advocated' seems a counsel of despair.

As for anticipating a beneficial effect of loans instead of grants for undergraduates on the basis of experience abroad, let us ponder the fact that recently at a European Conference the British government was able to assert (even to be proud of) the fact that British universities had a higher proportion of working-class students than anywhere else in Europe – where loans, not grants, prevail. We need to be far clearer about the issues, factors and effects involved in the matter of loans and grants, and these need the most careful analysis and consideration before action is even contemplated – there is no particular virtue in the inevitability of gradualness in the wrong direction. Meanwhile let intelligent progressive action be taken on the authors' major proposals listed at the outset of this comment, and see what this can effect *before* the question of loans versus grants is fully considered and decided.

Chapter Nine
Conclusion
Charles Carter

The authors of this book approach their subject from different angles, and reach different conclusions about the policies which should be followed. But it is important to note the matters on which we are agreed.

First, we agree that the large expansion in higher education during the 1970s, forecast by Richard Layard and Gareth Williams, is both inevitable and desirable. We have no room for arguments for restriction based on the belief that 'more means worse'. The *more* is the consequence of a spread of educational opportunity which brings into use talents which previously lay idle and wasted. Nor have we any sympathy for the view that higher education should not be expanded because there will not be enough jobs for those who come from universities and colleges. The job market is quite capable of adapting itself to a change in the educational system: on the experience of other countries (for instance, the United States) it will in fact adapt itself so as to use graduates and others with similar qualifications in jobs previously held by non-graduates. The results of this may be economically desirable. For instance, it would be helpful to have more well-trained scientists in production (as distinct from research) jobs. But even if it could be shown that the economic system has no need of any expansion of higher education, we would all still argue in favour of providing it. For surely education should be judged by its contribution to the quality of civilization and to the happiness and self-fulfilment of human beings. It is a poor, silly doctrine which looks at it only as an ancillary in the production of material wealth.

We agree, too, that the cost of the expansion will inevitably be substantial. There are many reasonable economies to be explored, but no one has found, and no one is likely to find, the secret of providing an acceptable quality of higher education at a dramatic reduction in cost. The cost levels actually achieved will depend on the mix of subjects, on the balance between teaching and research, on the quality of residence and social facilities for students, and on the scale of the sub-sections of each institution. These are the real factors, rather than the form of government of the institution: the decision whether to develop 'autonomous' or 'public sector' institutions cannot sensibly be made on cost grounds, unless it can be shown that a particular form of government necessarily and inevitably affects the *real* factors in the direction of high costs.

While we would all support a sensible concern with economy in higher education, we are conscious of the danger that, if too much attention is focused on costs, economy will be bought at the expense of quality. In particular, non-quantifiable benefits are all too easily traded for quantifiable savings. But we are not pessimistic about the public willingness to pay the costs of doing the job properly. Any government which fails to provide reasonable opportunities for those who are qualified for higher education will, we think, soon be subject to public pressure. Indeed, we shall not be surprised if the demand outruns the estimates given in this book.

In discussing future policy we are in agreement on one very important matter. All of us welcome the variety which exists in British higher education, and want to see it increase further – for instance, by the development in the polytechnics of new fields of study (p. 133), or by the creation of new kinds of college (p. 137). This agreement is perhaps surprising: first, because the British system is already one of the most varied and flexible in the world, and second, because an author coming from a particular type of institution might be expected to want the best features of the tradition with which he is familiar to become the standard for all. But we are all impressed by the extent of the differences, both in the background and previous training of students, and in their attitudes and vocational intentions. We see it as a strength.

Another reason for variety is the association of teaching with the other functions, often loosely summarized as 'research', but analysed with more care on pages 77–80. All of us regard an association of this kind as natural and desirable, but do not expect it to follow fixed rules. At one extreme there will continue to be institutions almost entirely concerned with teaching, having only such additional scholarly activity as is necessary to keep the teaching alive and relevant. At another extreme there might be institutions which are primarily research units, doing some teaching (perhaps of a very specialized kind) as a by-product of research. Between these extremes there lies an infinity of other combinations of activities, and there is no reason to think that the 'mix' traditionally thought best in universities is appropriate elsewhere. For that matter, the traditional university mix is itself a myth, for wide variations exist within and between universities. We see no reason why, within the whole field of higher education as well as within universities, new combinations of teaching with the associated activities should not be established.

Our main areas of disagreement are interesting and significant, for our divergence in matters of policy (illustrated in chapter 7) arises because we are not agreed on questions of fact. Putting it simply, Peter Venables and I do not recognize the universities we know as conforming, or likely in the future to conform, to the image presented by George Brosan in chapter 5; and George Brosan is equally at a loss in recognizing our idea of the nature and limitations of a polytechnic. A disagreement on facts ought to be easily resolved, but this one is a little more stubborn. It arises in part because it is not easy to be sure, in all the variety presented by each kind of institution, just what is important or 'representative'; but in part also because we are all to some extent guessing about the future. What will the polytechnics really be like when they are fully established and have had time to develop new areas of study? What will the universities be like when a much larger proportion of their total numbers is to be found in the ex-CATs and the new foundations? The relationship between vocational interests, the needs of employment, and the claims of pure scholarship enters into the argument at several points; but this relationship is difficult to analyse, even in the actions and views of a single individual. Over quite a short period of time the relationship seen to be 'normal' within a particular part of an institution may change substantially. Perhaps it is not surprising that, looking at the colours of a complex and changing scene, we paint different pictures.

By presenting our alternative appreciations we face the reader with the questions which have to be answered. The British system of higher education is no doubt capable of being developed in two or more cooperating systems of institutions, separated by function; though Peter Venables and I would dispute an assertion that a clear separation already exists. Equally, it is no doubt capable of being developed as a single comprehensive system; though George Brosan would question whether this would encourage the right sort of variety of attitude and function. The choice has to be made, and will not be well made by a process of drift and avoidance of decision. We believe that it should be made by a rational consideration of the facts and the issues that we have set out, *having due regard to the time required to implement change*. For in education the time-scale for achieving a planned change is exceptionally long, and decisions on many major matters are therefore required in the near future. These decisions are not just administrative or economic, they are also academic (some, indeed, are *primarily* academic) – and they have to be woven into a complex, and already changing, educational and institutional pattern. We hope this book will help to produce wise choices and decisions for the coming period of challenge and opportunity.

Other Penguin Education Specials

The New Polytechnics: The People's Universities

Eric E. Robinson

Challenged from below by an increasing tide of student unrest, harassed from above by economic pressures, the universities – amongst the last strongholds of elitist education – seem unlikely to survive in their present form for very much longer.

'Sooner or later,' writes Eric Robinson, 'this country must face a comprehensive reform of education beyond school – a reform that will bring higher education out of the ivory towers and make it available for all.'

The author traces the developments of higher education since the war, and argues that the divisions between university and technical college are indefensible on economic, social and political grounds. The new polytechnics which the Department of Education and Science are proposing to establish could, by bringing together academic, vocational, full- and part-time students, become higher education's equivalent of the comprehensive school.

The Impact of Robbins

Richard Layard, John King, Claus Moser

In 1963 the Robbins Report launched the most massive
expansion of higher education ever seen in Britain. The aim was to
create a new deal for the nation's talented young.

Yet today the chances of a sixth-former getting a place at a British
university are, if anything, slightly less than they were before the
Report, and it is in the fields of teacher training and further
education that the most significant expansions have taken place.
Future trends point the same way.

Did Robbins succeed? Here the leaders of the team that did the
research for that famous Report, Professor Claus Moser and Richard
Layard, and their colleague at the London School of Economics,
John King, look back over the past few years and explain what
happened to the ambitious blueprint for creating a broader system
of higher education in Britain.

Teaching and Learning in Higher Education

Ruth Beard

Provision for higher education is now recognized as a major social and educational need. In the United Kingdom alone, a million students by 1980 is no longer a wild statistic, but a realistic basis for forward planning. At the start of a new decade of expansion, Ruth Beard has produced a timely and comprehensive analysis of the nature of teaching and learning in higher education.

Drawing on innovations in teaching methods in universities and colleges, as well as on findings from educational research, Dr Beard examines ways in which the current upsurge of new ideas is affecting curricula, courses and teaching techniques. After a chapter on different psychological approaches to human learning, which sets out the theoretical background to the practical problems under discussion, the middle chapters of the book provide a rigorous analysis of the educational value of the lecture, the seminar, laboratory and small-group teaching.

The author, believing that courses cannot be fully effective unless teachers reconsider their methods in relation to their aims and objectives, evaluates important preliminary research which has looked at the interaction between teacher and student in different learning situations.

Teaching and Learning in Higher Education demonstrates the vital need to ensure further improvements in the quality of teaching during the coming years. The book will be of particular value to teachers in universities and colleges, and also to those who are likely to benefit most from the raising of standards – the students themselves.

Resources for Learning

L. C. Taylor

From all sides the traditional methods of classroom teaching are under pressure. They encourage passivity. They cannot easily cope with the range of abilities and interests found in most classes. They make hopelessly inefficient use of an already understaffed teaching force. In an education system which increasingly values individual learning, they are dangerously inflexible.

In this penetrating and highly original book, L. C. Taylor shows how the methods of education are inextricably related to the purpose we ascribe to it. If, for instance, we want a comprehensive system where children of different abilities learn together, then we must be prepared to devise new techniques to achieve this.

Drawing on his experience previously as headmaster of Sevenoaks School and now as Director of the Nuffield Resources for Learning Project, and also his researches in Russia, America and Sweden, L. C. Taylor examines critically the new techniques and instruments of classroom modernization, from individualized learning and team teaching, to computer-assisted instruction and closed-circuit television.

Education for Democracy

Edited by David Rubinstein and Colin Stoneman

The time for a radical manifesto on British education is long
overdue. For over twenty-five years the struggle to democratize our
system has been held back by those who see the proper function of
education as the production of an elite and, as the most efficient
means of effecting this, the labelling of children as A's or D's at the
earliest possible opportunity. Those children who do not meet the
requirements of the current elite have had some reason to be
disconsolate about their fate.

Here at last – appropriately at a time when the 'backlash' is
receiving all the attention, if not actually gaining the upper hand –
is a bold definition of the nature and purpose of 'education for
democracy'.

The contributors to this collection, all of whom have to grapple
daily with these problems on the lecture-hall or classroom floor, do
not attempt to put forward a single, easy solution. But whether they
are writing about the content of the primary curriculum or
university examinations, about slum schools or the new technology
of learning, there is one fundamental belief which they all hold in
common. They demand an education system which cares about *all*
children, regardless of race, class or intelligence, and which helps to
build a democratic society by upholding the qualities of compassion
and respect within its own walls.

Warwick University Ltd

Edited by E. P. Thompson

'In the conflict it became apparent that what was wrong was not a
close relationship with "industry" but a particular kind of
subordinate relationship with industrial capitalism – with an
industrial capitalism, moreover, which exerts its influence not only
directly in the councils of the University but also within the
educational organs of the State, and which, from both directions, is
demanding, for its better service, an approved educational product.'
E. P. Thompson

Warwick University Ltd is the story of how one university
uncovered and confronted this situation. It tells for the first time
the full story of the student unease that led to an invasion of the
Registry. In doing so it sets move and counter-move in the battle
of 'political files' against the major issues of privacy, academic
liberty and the public interest.

As we enter a new decade of expanding higher education, E. P.
Thompson and his colleagues set out to describe a real threat to
formal education and to the values that a 'learning society'
professes.